A Gospel Church Described
by Michael Harrison
with chapters by C. Matthew McMahon

Copyright Information

A Gospel Church Described, by Michael Harrison,
with chapters by C. Matthew McMahon, Ph.D., Th.D.
Edited by Therese B. McMahon

© 2026 by Puritan Publications and A Puritan's Mind

Published by Puritan Publications
A Ministry of A Puritan's Mind in Crossville, TN
www.apuritansmind.com
www.puritanpublications.com
www.reformedsynod.com
www.gracechapeltn.com

All rights reserved. No part of this publication may be reproduced, stored in a retrieval system or transmitted in any form by any means, electronic, mechanical, photocopy, recording or otherwise, without the prior permission of the publisher, except as provided by USA copyright law.

First Electronic Edition, 2026
First Modern Print Edition, 2026
Manufactured in the United States of America

eISBN: 978-1-62663-534-0
ISBN: 978-1-62663-535-7

Table of Contents

Clarity for a Confused Age 4
Meet Michael Harrison 17
Preface 22
To the Reader 24
The Introduction 29
Chapter 1: Names of the Church 33
Chapter 2: Membership 53
Chapter 3: Nature of the Church 67
Chapter 4: Ordination 107
Chapter 5: Member Duties 115
Chapter 6: Discipline 127
Chapter 7: Schism 138
Appendix: The Supper 149
Other Books by Michael Harrison at Puritan Publications 184

Clarity for a Confused Age
by C. Matthew McMahon, Ph.D. Th.D.

The church of Jesus Christ is no invention of man but the very kingdom of God *manifested* upon earth. The 1647 Westminster Confession (25.1) declares that "the catholic or universal Church, which is invisible, consists of the whole number of the elect, that have been, are, or shall be gathered into one, under Christ the Head thereof," (Ephesians 1:10, 22–23; Colossians 1:18). Here the eye is lifted beyond time and nation. The invisible church is the Father's eternal election embodied (Ephesians 1:4), the Son's purchase sealed (Ephesians 5:25–27), and the Spirit's work applied (2 Thessalonians 2:13). Known infallibly only to God (2 Timothy 2:19), it is unshakable, for its foundation is Christ Himself.

Following Scripture, the *Confession* insists also upon the visible church: "the kingdom of the Lord Jesus Christ, the house and family of God, out of which there is no ordinary possibility of salvation," (1 Corinthians 1:2; Acts 2:39; Matthew 28:19–20). This visible society is marked by Word and sacrament, ruled by Christ's ordinances, and populated by saints and hypocrites alike (Matthew 13:47). As Noah's ark bore both clean and unclean beasts, yet remained the vessel of deliverance (1 Peter 3:20–21), so the visible church is God's appointed means to preserve His people amidst a drowning world.

The Head of the church, both visible and invisible, *is Christ alone* (Ephesians 5:23; Colossians 1:18). No pope (Antichrist), council, or prelate may seize that crown (Matthew 23:8–10). The risen Christ "calls out of the world unto Himself, through the ministry of His Word, by His Spirit, those that are given unto Him by His Father," (John 10:16; John 12:32; Acts 2:47). He governs by officers of His choosing—pastors, teachers, elders, and deacons (Ephesians 4:11–12; Acts 20:28; 1 Timothy 3)—that His body might be edified, guarded, and fed.

This church is universal, stretching across all ages and nations (Psalm 2:8; Revelation 7:9). Yet she appears in particular congregations (Galatians 1:2; Revelation 1:4), where believers covenant together under Christ to worship, receive the ordinances, and walk in holy discipline (Matthew 18:17; Acts 2:42). Some churches are purer than others (Revelation 2–3), yet Christ preserves His own, promising that the gates of hell shall not prevail against her (Matthew 16:18).

Here, then, is the biblical church: chosen by the Father (Ephesians 1:4), redeemed by the Son (Acts 20:28), sanctified by the Spirit (1 Corinthians 12:13), governed by Christ's Word (Matthew 28:20), nourished by His ordinances (1 Corinthians 11:23–26), and preserved unto everlasting glory (Ephesians 5:27).

Now we turn to Michael Harrison (1640-1729). He belongs to the generation of *Puritan* and *Dissenting* divines who labored through one of the most turbulent periods of English church history. Though little is preserved of his personal life, the fragments that remain—gleaned from Calamy, Coleman, and scattered references—show him to be a faithful minister, a man unwilling to sacrifice conscience for conformity, and one determined to lay firm foundations for the people entrusted to his care. His work, *A Gospel Church Described* (this current work), stands as the fullest surviving testimony of his ecclesiology. It is a book written not for the schools but for the pews; not for speculative elaboration, but for the ordinary Christians of Potterspury, Caversfield, St. Ives, (his church) and beyond who needed plain direction in what it means to be a true church of Jesus Christ. With the confusion that the modern Evangelical Church has today of a Gospel Church, this work is paramount.

Harrison ministered during an age of fracture. *The Act of Uniformity* (1662) had expelled over two thousand ministers unwilling to bind conscience to imposed forms. Harrison himself preached in the parish church of Caversfield but, dissatisfied with the terms of conformity, withdrew and eventually established a dissenting congregation in Potterspury. From that base, he built a meeting house, pastored for nearly two decades, and then carried on his labors at St. Ives until his death in 1726. His life was one of quiet steadfastness rather than notoriety, but it is precisely in such hidden fidelity that the English church was preserved.

A Gospel Church Described was printed in London in 1700, during a moment of comparative liberty for dissenters. Harrison's preface acknowledges this indulgence and exhorts his people to live as grateful recipients of providential kindness. Yet liberty, he notes, had been abused by some: irregular preaching, unsound doctrine, and careless views of church order threatened to bring *reproach* upon the dissenting cause. This treatise, then, was his corrective—a concise, scripturally grounded account of what a true gospel church is.

Harrison organizes his description of a gospel church according to six categories: its author, its names, its head, its matter, its form, and its end. This framework allows him to proceed systematically, defining the church by Scripture's own language, distinguishing visible from invisible, catholic (universal) from particular, and drawing out the covenantal principles by which God gathers His people.

He treats ministry at length, addressing whether the church precedes the ministry or the ministry precedes the church. His answer is both biblically careful and pastorally wise: Christ appointed ministers before any church existed, sending them forth with His Word; yet the church is the ultimate end of that ministry, and the two belong inseparably together.

He distinguishes invisible and visible church: the invisible being the elect, united to Christ by faith and Spirit, known only to God; the visible being those who profess Christ and their children, joined in covenant fellowship. This distinction, long recognized in Reformed theology, he carefully explains with biblical warrant from Ephesians, 1 Peter, John, and other texts. On the matter of membership, Harrison devotes a full chapter to defending the inclusion of infants of believing parents as members of the visible church, appealing to the continuity of the covenant of grace from Abraham to Christ, to Deuteronomy's covenant renewal, to Acts 2:39, and to 1 Corinthians 7:14. His arguments reveal a thoroughly covenantal mind, echoing the mainstream Reformed conviction that baptism is the New Testament sign of covenant inclusion, replacing circumcision yet signifying the same grace.

Church discipline and schism are also addressed. Harrison distinguishes between necessary separation (when corrupt terms of communion are imposed) and sinful separation (when impatience with imperfection leads to division). His measured counsel reveals a pastoral concern to preserve both truth and love. To withdraw from sin is duty; to fracture the body without sufficient cause is rebellion.

An appendix has been added, *A Discourse on the Lord's Supper*, rooted in Numbers 9:13, reinforcing the seriousness of neglecting Christ's ordinances. Harrison insists that to absent oneself when duty requires is sin, for Christ's table is not optional but commanded.

Harrison's ecclesiology is not speculative but *exegetical*. His use of Matthew 16:18 ("upon this rock I will build my church") anchors his conviction that the church belongs to Christ and is indestructible against the gates of hell. His appeal to Ephesians 5 situates the church in the love of Christ, who gave Himself to present her spotless and glorious. His repeated citations of Acts 2, Acts 8, and 1 Corinthians 14–15 root membership, sacraments, and order in apostolic practice.

The covenant of grace is his interpretive key. For Harrison (and all good theologians), the Abrahamic covenant continues under the gospel, expanded to include the Gentiles, never repealed, but brought to clearer light. In this way, infants remain within its bounds, baptism seals its promise, and the visible church spans generations. Romans 11's olive tree is central: branches broken off for unbelief, Gentiles grafted in, one root nourishing all.

Numbers 9 and Isaiah 55 extend his biblical reach: the former a warning against neglect of ordinances, the latter an invitation to free grace. His doctrine is not an abstract system but a deeply scriptural mosaic, every part drawing from explicit biblical texts.

Harrison's treatise exemplifies classic reformed ecclesiology at the turn of the 18th century. It shares much with contemporaries like Owen, Goodwin, and the Independents, yet is shorter, plainer, and directed to common readers (as all his writings are). His insistence on order without rigidity, liberty without license, and covenant inclusion without presumption reveals a balanced mind. He avoided the extremes of formalism on one hand and enthusiasm on the other.

For the student of historical theology, Harrison's work illuminates the lived concerns of dissenting congregations: Who may preach? Who belongs to the church? What marks a true church? When is separation justified? These were not abstract disputes but pressing pastoral questions in an age of tolerated dissent, fragile liberty, and constant suspicion.

Modern readers will find in Harrison's little book *an antidote to confusion*. In a day when "church" is often reduced to a building, a brand, or a social association, Harrison insists that it is Christ's blood-bought assembly, covenanted with God, governed by His Word, gathered around His ordinances, and oriented toward His glory. His rejection of irregular preaching, his defense of covenant children, his care to distinguish true and false separation—all speak directly into present controversies.

The strength of his work lies in its *plainness*. He did not write for the academy but for the shoemaker who hid a pulpit in his wagon, for the farmer who gathered in a converted barn, for ordinary saints trying to live as Christ's flock. That is why this work deserves republication: because it remains what it was in 1700—a guide to the ordinary Christian who longs to know what Christ requires of His church.

A Gospel Church Described is a voice from a faithful shepherd of three centuries past, still summoning the flock of Christ to faithfulness. It is covenantal, biblical, and practical. It grounds the church not in the fancies of men but in the eternal purposes of God. To read it is to be instructed in the foundations of ecclesiology, to be warned against error, to be invited to grace, and to be exhorted to walk in holiness.

Scholars will value its window into dissenting thought; pastors will value its clarity on church order; believers will value its plain teaching on what it means to belong to Christ's body. Harrison's words, though simple, still resound: the church is Christ's, and Christ is jealous for her purity.

The church of Jesus Christ has never been man's invention. It is not the product of councils, committees, or clever strategies. It is the bride for whom the Son of God shed His blood, the household of faith, the temple of the Spirit, the pillar and ground of the truth. To misunderstand the church is to misunderstand one of the central purposes of redemption. To despise the church is to despise the very body of Christ. How can one say they love Jesus but not love his church?

What will you, reader, find personally in these pages? You will find Christ Himself at the center. Harrison begins with the names and titles of the church from Scripture—Christ's spouse, God's people, a holy nation, the house of the living God. He reminds us that the church is not an institution of men but a society of souls called out by God, bound to Him by covenant, joined to one another by love.

You will find careful teaching on the invisible and visible church. The invisible church is God's elect, known perfectly only to Him, united to Christ by Spirit and faith. The visible church is the society of those who profess Christ, together with their children. Here Harrison presses the covenant promises: the same covenant that embraced Abraham and his seed now embraces believers and their households. Infants, he shows from Genesis, Deuteronomy, Acts, and

Corinthians, are not excluded under the gospel. This is good news for weary parents: God still says, "I will be a God unto thee, and to thy seed after thee."

You will find practical wisdom on ministry. Without preaching, there is no faith; without faith, no church. Ministry is God's appointed instrument for building His house. That is why unauthorized preachers are *dangerous*, and why those who step into the pulpit without the call or gift wound both themselves and their hearers. Jude calls them "brute beasts" (Jude v. 10).

You will find sober counsel on discipline and schism. Churches may be imperfect—Corinth was filled with factions, Galatia with confusion, Sardis with deadness, Laodicea with lukewarmness—yet they remained churches of Christ. Imperfection does not cancel Christ's ownership. But when sin is embraced as law, when communion is fenced with terms God never gave, then separation may become duty. Harrison treads carefully, urging believers not to abandon love, yet warning them to stand fast in truth.

You will find serious exhortations about the ordinances. The Lord's Supper is not optional. To refuse it when called is sin. Numbers 9:13 warns of being cut off for neglect. Harrison holds both together: the Supper is duty, but it is also invitation. Come, for Christ welcomes; come, for Christ commands.

Why should you, a modern reader, care about a dissenting pastor from 1700? Because the questions he faced are the questions we still face. What is the church? Who belongs to it? What makes a true minister? When should I stay, and when must I leave? How should I approach the Lord's Table? These are not relics of history but *daily realities* for the people of God.

The current climate of Evangelicalism is reduced to livestreams, marketing, or casual associations. Harrison calls us back to Scripture. He reminds us that the church is not ours to invent but *Christ's to define*. He tells us that covenant promises still hold, that ordinances still bind, that ministers still matter, and that the body of Christ is still precious.

If you are weary of confusion, come learn from a pastor who sought clarity. If you long for assurance that your children belong to God, come hear the covenant promises re-stated. If you wonder how to discern true ministry, come see the pattern laid out. If you have grown careless about worship, come be reminded that Christ's ordinances are not trifles but treasures.

Harrison closes his preface showing that his people might have sound judgment, holiness of life, peace with God, peace of conscience, growth in grace, and an abundant entrance into the everlasting kingdom of Christ. That is the prayer of every faithful shepherd. It is the prayer of this book for you.

So read on—not as a relic of the past, but as a living word of instruction. Read to know what it means to belong to Christ's church. Read to be guarded from error, guided in truth, and grounded in grace. Read, and rejoice that Christ has *not left* His people in confusion, but still speaks through His *true servants*, calling His flock to walk together in covenant love until the day when the church militant becomes the church triumphant.

In Christ's grace and mercy,
C. Matthew McMahon, Ph.D., Th.D.
From My study, September, 2025
"...search the Scriptures..." (John 5:39).
www.apuritansmind.com
www.puritanpublications.com
www.gracechapeltn.com
www.reformedsynod.com

Meet Michael Harrison
By C. Matthew McMahon, Ph.D., Th.D.

There is no full biography of Rev. Michael Harrison (1640-1729). What we know of him comes from fragments in works by Edmund Calamy, Thomas Coleman and other writers making mention of him in conjunction with historic information on Edmund Calamy. He was born around 1640 and appears to have been part of the Bard family of Caversfield, (possibly through marriage). We do not have a record of his early years, or his schooling.

We do find the labors of Rev. Harrison mentioned in a church in the parish Church of Caversfield, Bucks. He preached regularly there and resided in the vicarage. Coleman says of him that he "performed the duties of a faithful minister of Christ for a number of years." Harrison became dissatisfied with the terms of conformity. Instead, he maintained familiar connection with evangelical *dissenters*, and finally became fully prepared to recede from the Church of England.

Dr. Edmund Calamy, who was then studying at Oxford, says, "There were at this time monthly fasts appointed by authority, and generally observed very regularly, to implore the divine blessing, in order to the success of our forces. At one of these fasts I was at Bicester, and assisted old Mr. Cornish, who was indisposed, at his Meeting House, in the morning; and afterwards walked over to Caversfield, about a mile distant, the Dissenters in a body bearing me company. There I preached in the public Church in the afternoon, and had a crowded Church from the country round. Mr. Michael Harrison preached in the Church, of which Mr. Beard was patron; and he lived in the house adjoining. But Mr. Harrison was now away from home, in Northamptonshire, where he was gathering a congregation of Dissenters about Potterspury, designing to quit the Church and settle among them."

Harrison's efforts were successful; he soon gathered around him some friends, removed to reside among them, formed a Congregational Church, and purchased a property, on which he fitted up a place of worship. He was the Minster at Caversfield Parish on the Buckinghamshire/Oxfordshire border up to 1690.

When Harrison moved to Pury, a Mr. John Warr, who formerly lived in the neighborhood of Caversfield, came with him to enjoy the benefit of his ministry. And connected with this circumstance is another, which will show something of the spirit of the times. Coleman makes note, "When Mr. Harrison came to Pury, he brought a pulpit with him, which he deemed it necessary to conceal; therefore, to prevent it being known, Mr. Warr, being a shoemaker, contrived to fill it with shoe-pegs, and brought it among his own goods in a wagon from Bicester."

Harrison's wife owned some property and Harrison used the proceeds of that sale to enable them to purchase the premises on which his dwelling-house and the Church Meeting House were built. When the barn which formed the *humble Meeting House* was prepared, at the request of the people, Dr. Calamy preached at the opening, with a large crowd. In making this move, Harrison trusted in the God who provides, and his faithfulness to bring about true reform to the people of the area for the glory of Christ. Calamy noted in his, "History of His Own Time," that Harrison was a minister of this congregation initially in the Church of England, but later succeeded to the Presbyterian Church.

Harrison labored in this newly established non-conformist church in Potterspury until 1709, for about nineteen years. Afterwards, Harrison moved and became the minister of a Church at St. Ives (a puritan stronghold), in the county of Huntingdon. There too he labored for many years, and died in January, 1726.

His only known works are (all Published by Puritan Publications):

1. *Christ's Righteousness Imputed, or the Glorious Doctrine of Free Justification by the Imputation of the Pure and Spotless Righteousness of Jesus Christ*, 1690. (Republished by Puritan Publications).
2. *Infant Baptism God's Ordinance*, 1694. (Republished by Puritan Publications).
3. *The Best Match, or, The Believer's Marriage with Christ*, 1690. (This Current Work). Originally printed in London, for Nathanael Ranew, at the king's-arms in St. Paul's church-yard, 1691.
4. *A Gospel Church Described* in its author, names, head, matter, form, and end wherein are various cases concerning the ministry, divination, admission of members, discipline, schism ... / by Michael Harrison in Potters-Pury, 1700.

For further study:

"Memorials of The Independent Churches in Northamptonshire; With Biographical Notices of Their Pastors, and Some Account of the Puritan Ministers Who Laboured in the County," by Thomas Coleman; Calamy's,

"An Historical Account of My Own Life, with Some Reflections, Volume 1;" "Poems by Robert Wilde with a Historical and Biographical Pref. and Notes," By John Hunt; "The Western Antiquary, Volume 8," edited by William Henry Kearley Wright.

Preface

To the Christian and Candid Reader, Especially the Flock Over Which the Holy Ghost Has Appointed Me Overseer...

A gospel church is set forth in this work, described according to its author, its names, its head, its matter, its form, and its end. Within these pages, various matters are addressed concerning the ministry, including the ordination of ministers, the admission of church members, the exercise of church discipline, and the nature of schism. Consideration is also given to whether laymen may preach or be heard without committing sin. Many other subjects are treated, all contributing to a clear and right understanding of the nature of a true church, among other things.

Additionally, this work includes a discourse on the Lord's Supper, grounded in the text of Numbers 9:13, which declares, "But the man that is clean, and is not in a journey, and forbeareth to keep the passover, even the same soul shall be cut off from among his people: because he brought not the offering of the LORD in his appointed season, that man shall bear his sin." This passage shows the solemn duty of partaking in the Lord's Supper, warning against neglect of this sacred ordinance.

To the Reader

The epistle to the Christian and candid reader, more especially that flock over which the holy ghost hath made me overseer.

Dear Friends,

    The Lord has shown His gracious favor to His afflicted people in this nation by inclining the hearts of our rulers to grant them liberty in matters where their consciences could not comfortably conform. This indulgence, I am confident, will bring everlasting honor to our present sovereign, the most excellent of kings, upon whom the eyes of all Protestant churches and nations are fixed with great expectation of continued blessings. Likewise, honor is due to our noble patriots who have established this liberty through the enactment of law.

It is now our solemn duty to conduct ourselves with all reverence and submission to the present government. We must not behave like ungrateful children who harm the hand that feeds them, for this liberty is a precious gift, like milk from a nurturing breast.

It is, however, all too clear that some individuals, if not driven by *malicious* intent, are at least *weak and thoughtless*, misusing this liberty by spreading unsound doctrines and engaging in irregular and unbiblical practices. Those who deliberately pursue such practices, as it is to be feared some do, with the intent to undermine the cause of dissenters and provoke the revocation of our liberty, I leave to be dealt with by others, for I have little hope of correcting them. Such persons are but Protestants in *disguise*, hiding their true motives.

Yet there are others who err through weakness or ignorance, and though their actions may sometimes be misguided, their intentions are *sincere*. For these, there is hope of amendment, and it is partly for their benefit that this treatise on the nature of a gospel church is written. It would greatly promote the peace and welfare of Christian congregations if young believers would pay greater attention to the state of their own hearts and strive to establish a foundation of sound principles, becoming well-versed in the essential truths of the Christian faith. How often do we encounter those who speak loftily of spiritual experiences and communion with God, yet remain woefully ignorant of the plain and fundamental doctrines of religion?

To the Reader

A right understanding of the nature of a gospel church would greatly aid Christians *in discerning their proper roles and responsibilities,* as well as what *God* requires of them as members of His body. As for this present treatise, I acknowledge that its style is plain, its structure imperfect, and its presentation unrefined. Yet it may still prove useful to those for whom it is intended: namely, those who lack the means to purchase, the time to read, or the ability to comprehend larger and more scholarly works. Brief summaries, though simple, are not without value, for, as the saying goes, *vita brevis est, ars longa* (life is short, but the pursuit of knowledge is long). Even the heathen philosopher Seneca observed, *magnam esse dementiam, etc.* (it is great folly, in the brevity of time, to pursue superfluous knowledge).

This work is primarily intended for my own congregation, most of whom are occupied with callings that afford them little time for extensive reading. They will read this brief treatise, whereas a longer work might be overlooked. I am not overly concerned with the opinions of others regarding myself or this work. Those who find it displeasing are free to set it aside and, if they wish, produce something better in their own time. To avoid giving offense, I must assure the reader that nothing in this work is intended to provoke or stir controversy, though *some* may perceive it otherwise.

I anticipate that two groups may take offense at my words:

The Anabaptists, because I have demonstrated, from the unity and continuity of God's covenant, that infants have a right to church membership and baptism. Yet let me assure my brethren of this persuasion that, as I love all men as fellow creatures, I hold a particular affection for those among them who are sound in other fundamental doctrines and live as serious, godly Christians. Though we differ on this point, I regard them as true Christians and fellow members of the body of Christ, united in the essentials of faith.

Lay preachers and their supporters and followers,[1] because I have shown the error of their engaging in a work to which God has neither called nor equipped them. Yet they have no more reason to be angry with me than a man with a broken bone or dislocated joint would have to be angry with a friend who, in kindness, offers to set the bone or heal the wound. What I have written is out of pity and compassion for their souls. If they refuse to hear, I will not cease to pity them and pray for their repentance and

---

[1] Non-denominational preachers, churches and people.

enlightenment. I earnestly desire for all people soundness of judgment, holiness of heart and life, peace with God, peace in their consciences, an increase of grace in this life, and an abundant entrance into the everlasting kingdom of our Lord and Savior Jesus Christ hereafter, "to whom we must give account," (Hebrews 13:17).

So prays your soul's friend, in our dearest Lord,

From my study in Potters-Pury,
May 15, 1700.
MICHAEL HARRISON

The Introduction

If the Lord Jesus Christ was so captivated by the beauty and holiness of His church, even when she was under a legal and less glorious dispensation, that He passionately longed for and desired her fellowship—as expressed in the words, "Thou hast ravished my heart, my sister, my spouse; thou hast ravished my heart with one of thine eyes, with one chain of thy neck. How fair is thy love, my sister, my spouse! how much better is thy love than wine! and the smell of thine ointments than all spices! Thy lips, O my spouse, drop as the honeycomb: honey and milk are under thy tongue; and the smell of thy garments is like the smell of Lebanon," (Song of Solomon 4:9-11), and again, "His lips are like lilies, dropping sweet smelling myrrh," (Song of Solomon 5:13)—then how much more must His love have moved Him! This love led Him to descend into a state of incarnation, humiliation, and death, that He might redeem His church and make all her members "kings and priests unto God and his Father; to him be glory and dominion for ever and ever. Amen," (Revelation 1:6). Through the merits of His sufferings, He presents this church to God as "a glorious church, not having spot, or wrinkle, or any such thing; but that it should be holy and without blemish," (Ephesians 5:27).

If Christ loves His church with such fervent devotion, it must surely be a most pleasant and delightful task to *inquire* into the nature and characteristics of this church. Now, in the gospel dispensation, she has cast off the veil of the old covenant and stands in the clear light of the gospel, having reached her full maturity and adorned with the glorious robes of Christ's righteousness, far more beautiful than ever before.

This inquiry is, all the more necessary because, though we live in an age blessed with the light of the gospel, many still stumble in darkness, particularly concerning the *true nature of a gospel church*. It is a sorrowful sight to observe the strange errors into which men fall and the misguided notions some hold about the church. On one hand, there are those who continually cry out, "The church, the church; we are sons of the church!" Yet, by this, they often mean either a mere building of wood and stone where the church gathers to worship God or a collection of unscriptural traditions *devised by men* and *imposed upon tender consciences*. But the church of God is something far more excellent than either of these.

On the other hand, there are those who claim to possess greater spiritual attainments than others, imagining a church on earth that exists only in heaven. Carried aloft by fervent zeal and passionate affections, but lacking the foundation of sound knowledge, they are without the solid principles needed to guide them in God's ways. Though their sails are filled with the wind of enthusiasm, their lack of balanced judgment leaves them vulnerable to being overturned by every temptation.

I humbly submit that if we could find a way to correct these mistaken notions about the nature of a gospel church, it would be a powerful means to resolve our differences. An agreement in that article of our creed—"I believe in the holy catholic church"—would work wonders in uniting us in harmony and peace. If we could reach an amicable consensus on this point, I am confident that any remaining differences on other matters would not destroy Christian love or disrupt the unity and peace of the church.

This, therefore, is the purpose of this modest endeavor now placed in your hands, written by one who is no partisan in religion but bears a universal love and tenderness for *Christians* of all denominations. If I err in any way, it is not out of favoritism toward one group over another, nor from a lack of effort to discern the truth, nor from a lack of love for the truth, but solely from the unavoidable frailty of my human nature.

Chapter 1: Names of the Church

The church is considered under the following headings: 1. Its names. 2. Its nature. 3. Whether the church or the ministry is first in the order of nature. 4. The distinction between the church invisible and visible, and related matters.

First. Let us first examine the church in the names, titles, and descriptions given to it in holy Scripture. Our Savior calls it, in Matthew 16:18, "my church," saying, "And I say also unto thee, That thou art Peter, and upon this rock I will build my church; and the gates of hell shall not prevail against it," (Matthew 16:18). The Greek word used here, ἐκκλησία (ekklesia), signifies an assembly called together, derived from the Hebrew word *kahal*, which means to be gathered or congregated. The term "church" carries several meanings in Scripture:

1. It refers to any multitude gathered together in one place for any purpose, as in Acts 19:32, where it is written, "Some therefore cried one thing, and some another: for the assembly was confused; and the more part knew not wherefore they were come together" (Acts 19:32). Here, ἐκκλησία is used for a confused gathering.

2. It is used for a company of malignant or wicked men, as in Psalm 26:5, "I have hated the congregation of evil doers; and will not sit with the wicked," (Psalm 26:5), where the Hebrew *kahal* is employed.
3. It denotes Christians assembled together for the worship of God, as in 1 Corinthians 14:34, "Let your women keep silence in the churches: for it is not permitted unto them to speak; but they are commanded to be under obedience, as also saith the law."
4. It refers to the glorified saints in heaven, as in Hebrews 12:23, "To the general assembly and church of the firstborn, which are written in heaven, and to God the Judge of all, and to the spirits of just men made perfect."
5. It signifies the rulers and pastors of the church, distinct from the congregation, as in Matthew 18:17, "And if he shall neglect to hear them, tell it unto the church: but if he neglect to hear the church, let him be unto thee as an heathen man and a publican." Here, "church" refers to the pastors and rulers in whom governing authority is vested.

6. It denotes the faithful within a single household, as in Romans 16:5, "Likewise greet the church that is in their house."
7. It applies to a particular congregation, including both *rulers* and *members*, pastor and people, as in Revelation 2:1, "Unto the angel of the church of Ephesus write."

The term "church" is now commonly used to signify a society that stands in a covenant relationship with God as His people, whether they are, gathered together in assemblies or are apart, encompassing both the universal society of God's people—the whole church—and particular congregations as parts of that whole.

Furthermore, the church is given other titles and descriptions in Scripture:

1. The people of God, as in 1 Peter 2:10, "Which in time past were not a people, but are now the people of God: which had not obtained mercy, but now have obtained mercy."
2. The sons of God, as in Genesis 6:2, "That the sons of God saw the daughters of men that they were fair; and they took them wives of all which they chose." and 1 John 3:1-2, "Behold, what manner of love the Father hath bestowed upon us, that we should be

called the sons of God: therefore the world knoweth us not, because it knew him not. Beloved, now are we the sons of God."

3. A righteous nation that keeps the truth, as in Isaiah 26:2, "Open ye the gates, that the righteous nation which keepeth the truth may enter in."

4. The saints of the Most High, as in Daniel 7:18, "But the saints of the most High shall take the kingdom, and possess the kingdom for ever, even for ever and ever."

5. A chaste virgin, the spouse of Christ, as in 2 Corinthians 11:2, "For I am jealous over you with godly jealousy: for I have espoused you to one husband, that I may present you as a chaste virgin to Christ," and the wife of the Lamb, that is, of Christ, as in Revelation 19:7, "Let us be glad and rejoice, and give honour to him: for the marriage of the Lamb is come, and his wife hath made herself ready."

6. The house of the living God, as in 1 Timothy 3:15, "But if I tarry long, that thou mayest know how thou oughtest to behave thyself in the house of God, which is the church of the living God, the pillar and ground of the truth."

7. A chosen generation, a royal priesthood, a holy nation, a peculiar people, as in 1 Peter 2:9, "But ye are a chosen generation, a royal priesthood, an holy nation, a peculiar people; that ye should shew forth the praises of him who hath called you out of darkness into his marvellous light," along with many other titles.

II. Let us now consider the nature of this church. It is not a worldly but a spiritual society, united not by human or civil bonds but by sacred ties, not for earthly purposes but for the glory of God, the spiritual edification of its members, and their eternal salvation. To better understand the nature of this *heavenly society*, the church, we must examine it under the various distinctions by which it is commonly presented: as invisible or visible, triumphant or militant, catholic (universal) or particular.

III. Before addressing these distinctions, let us shed light on a question often raised: whether the church or the ministry is first in the order of nature. Some have supposed that a pastor of a church must first be a member of that church, implying that the church precedes the ministry. But if this were so, how could the church itself come into being? The preaching of the gospel is the means appointed by God to convert souls to Christ and thereby establish churches, as it is written, "So then faith cometh by hearing, and hearing by the word of God," (Romans 10:17). Without a ministry, it is difficult to see how churches could exist according to this order. Christ established a gospel ministry before any church was formed; He sent out the apostles and the seventy disciples, as recorded in Luke 9:1-2, "Then he called his twelve disciples together, and gave them power and authority over all devils, and to cure diseases. And he sent them to preach the kingdom of God, and to heal the sick," and Luke 10:1, "After these things the Lord appointed other seventy also, and sent them two and two before his face into every city and place, whither he himself would come." These went forth preaching the gospel, converting many to Christ, who were later gathered into churches. In this way, while the church is the ultimate purpose of the ministry and, in God's design, precedes it, *a ministry* may exist before a church is formed. The church is gathered and established through the ministry of the Word, and ministers may, and sometimes must, be set apart by *solemn ordination* before they are attached to a *particular* church, preaching the gospel to convert souls to Christ. I will speak further on the nature of the gospel ministry later.

    IV. Now let us consider the church as invisible or visible.

1. Let us examine the nature of the invisible church. The invisible church consists of the whole number of the elect, effectually called by God out of a state of sin to faith in Christ through the Word and Spirit of God, according to His good pleasure. They are united to Christ, their spiritual head, through which they receive grace in this life and glory in the life to come, all to the praise and glory of God's free grace.

In this description of the invisible church, observe the following: 1. The author, 2. The matter, 3. The form, 4. The head, 5. The end of the church.

1. The author is God—Father, Son, and Holy Spirit. God the Father elects and ordains His people to eternal life as the end and to holiness as the means to that end, as it is written, "According as he hath chosen us in him before the foundation of the world, that we should be holy and without blame before him in love," (Ephesians 1:4). The Lord Jesus Christ redeems us from sin and hell by His precious blood, as in Ephesians 1:7, "In whom we have redemption through his blood, the forgiveness of sins, according to the riches of his grace." The Holy Spirit sanctifies us, unites us to Christ, and prepares us for heaven.

2. The matter of the invisible church consists of elected and truly regenerated believers. While a credible profession of faith is sufficient for *membership* in the visible church, nothing less than *true union* with Christ qualifies one for the invisible church. The elect, before they believe, are members only in God's decree, as in 2 Thessalonians 2:13, "But we are bound to give thanks alway to God for you, brethren beloved of the Lord, because God hath from the beginning chosen you to salvation through sanctification of the Spirit and belief of the truth." Likewise, 1 Peter 2:5 states, "Ye also, as lively stones, are built up a spiritual house, an holy priesthood, to offer up spiritual sacrifices, acceptable to God by Jesus Christ." In this way, only elect, converted believers form the matter of the *invisible* church.

3. The form of the invisible church is the union by which its elect, believing members are joined to Christ, their head. The bond of this union, which constitutes the form of the invisible church, is the Holy Spirit and faith. By the Holy Spirit, God directly works in the heart, as in Ezekiel 36:27, "And I will put my spirit within you, and cause you to walk in my statutes, and ye shall keep my judgments,

and do them," and Ephesians 2:22, "In whom ye also are builded together for an habitation of God through the Spirit." By faith, the believer's invisible hand, the believer lays hold of Christ and is united to Him, as in John 17:21, "That they all may be one; as thou, Father, art in me, and I in thee, that they also may be one in us: that the world may believe that thou hast sent me," and Ephesians 3:17, "That Christ may dwell in your hearts by faith; that ye, being rooted and grounded in love." By love, believers are united to one another, as in John 13:35, "By this shall all men know that ye are my disciples, if ye have love one to another."

4. The head of this church is Christ, as in Ephesians 1:10, "That in the dispensation of the fulness of times he might gather together in one all things in Christ, both which are in heaven, and which are on earth; even in him," and Ephesians 1:22, "And hath put all things under his feet, and gave him to be the head over all things to the church," and Ephesians 5:23, "For the husband is the head of the wife, even as Christ is the head of the church: and he is the saviour of the body."

5. The end of the church is twofold: supreme and subordinate. The supreme end is *the glory of God's free grace and mercy,* as in Ephesians 1:5-6, "Having predestinated us unto the adoption of children by Jesus Christ to himself, according to the good pleasure of his will, To the praise of the glory of his grace, wherein he hath made us accepted in the beloved." The subordinate end is the salvation and eternal blessedness of the church and every member, as in 2 Thessalonians 2:13-14, "But we are bound to give thanks alway to God for you, brethren beloved of the Lord, because God hath from the beginning chosen you to salvation through sanctification of the Spirit and belief of the truth: Whereunto he called you by our gospel, to the obtaining of the glory of our Lord Jesus Christ."

The church, thus considered, is called *invisible*, not as men, but as elect and chosen by God. Though their persons are visible, their effectual calling, grace, holiness, and union with Christ are invisible. As men, they are seen by others; as saints, they are known only to the Lord Christ, as in 2 Timothy 2:19, "Nevertheless the foundation of God standeth sure, having this seal, The Lord knoweth them that are his. And, Let every one that nameth the name of Christ depart from iniquity." In this sense, the church is "a garden inclosed, a spring shut up, a fountain sealed," (Song of Solomon 4:12).

However, the church, as in this way considered, is not the standard for *gathering* or *planting* churches or admitting members. If we were to join only with churches composed entirely of true saints united to Christ by living faith, we would never join any church or would need to separate from all churches on earth, for the church, as invisible, has always been, is, and will remain invisible in this world.

The invisible church may also be considered as triumphant or militant, universal (catholic) or particular.

1. The invisible church is called triumphant when part of it has reached heaven, triumphing with Christ, having gained complete victory over the world, the flesh, and the devil. This triumphant church consists of the spirits of just men made perfect, together with the blessed angels, as in Hebrews 12:22-23, "But ye are come unto mount Sion, and unto the city of the living God, the heavenly Jerusalem, and to an innumerable company of angels, To the general assembly and church of the firstborn, which are written in heaven, and to God the Judge of all, and to

the spirits of just men made perfect." Likewise, Revelation 7:9-15 describes, "After this I beheld, and, lo, a great multitude, which no man could number, of all nations, and kindreds, and people, and tongues, stood before the throne, and before the Lamb, clothed with white robes, and palms in their hands; And cried with a loud voice, saying, Salvation to our God which sitteth upon the throne, and unto the Lamb... These are they which came out of great tribulation, and have washed their robes, and made them white in the blood of the Lamb."

2. The church is called *militant* when part of it remains in this world, in a suffering condition, fighting under the cross of Christ against the world, the flesh, and the devil. Sufferings are the usual lot of God's church in this vale of misery, as Christ said, "And he said to them all, If any man will come after me, let him deny himself, and take up his cross daily, and follow me," (Luke 9:23). And, "We must through much tribulation enter into the kingdom of God," (Acts 14:22). Yet God is graciously present with His militant church, as in Isaiah 43:1-3, "But now thus saith the LORD that created thee, O Jacob, and he that formed thee, O Israel, Fear not: for I have

redeemed thee, I have called thee by thy name; thou art mine. When thou passest through the waters, I will be with thee; and through the rivers, they shall not overflow thee: when thou walkest through the fire, thou shalt not be burned; neither shall the flame kindle upon thee. For I am the LORD thy God, the Holy One of Israel, thy Saviour."

3. The church is called *catholic* because it is not confined to one family, kingdom, or nation. While a particular church or pastor may be termed catholic in respect of soundness of doctrine, here the term signifies the church as encompassing believers from every nation in the world who belong to Christ (universal), "And the times of this ignorance God winked at; but now commandeth all men every where to repent," (Acts 17:30), and, "Then Peter opened his mouth, and said, Of a truth I perceive that God is no respecter of persons: But in every nation he that feareth him, and worketh righteousness, is accepted with him," (Acts 10:34-35). The church, in this way considered, extends to all times and places and is one church, the *mystical* or *spiritual body* of Christ, having one faith, one hope, one baptism, one rule, and enjoying the same salvation, as in 1

Corinthians 1:17, "For Christ sent me not to baptize, but to preach the gospel: not with wisdom of words, lest the cross of Christ should be made of none effect." And, "There is one body, and one Spirit, even as ye are called in one hope of your calling; One Lord, one faith, one baptism, One God and Father of all, who is above all, and through all, and in you all," (Ephesians 4:4-6).

4. The church is *particular* when the universal catholic church is divided into smaller societies, consisting of as many as can conveniently meet together in one place to worship God unitedly. Such were the churches mentioned in the New Testament, such as those at Corinth, Ephesus, Philippi, and others. But I will first address the church as visible before proceeding further with the description of particular churches.

II. Visible: When we say the church is *invisible* or *visible*, it must not be thought that there are two distinct churches, one invisible and one visible. Rather, it is the same church considered in *different respects*: invisible in one sense and visible in another. The Lord Plessis, a gentleman of France, in his treatise on the church, aptly stated, "We will commit unto God, the searcher of hearts, the knowledge of the invisible church, and will content ourselves to search for the visible in God's Word; into which all must in this life retire themselves, which desire to be gathered into the invisible church in the world to come." Nevertheless, we note the difference between the two: the invisible church contains only the regenerate, while the visible church includes *both* the regenerate and the unregenerate; the invisible church comprises only the elect, while the visible church includes all who are brought into it by the preaching of the gospel.

Now let us consider the nature of the visible church.

Definition: The *visible* church is the society of all those who profess Christianity and regeneration and are joined externally to Christ and to one another by the profession of faith and love, together with their children.
As before, we consider the author, matter, form, head, and end of the visible church.

1. The author of the church, both invisible and visible, is the same holy God who has instituted and appointed it and who gathers it by the preaching of the Word. Some are united to Christ by a saving union, while others are joined by an outward and visible profession.

2. The matter of the visible church consists of all who profess Christianity and regeneration, together with their children. Though not all may be true Christians or truly regenerated, those who make a credible profession are part of the visible church.

Here, three points must be considered:

1. All true Christians, regenerated by the Word and Spirit and united to Christ by faith, are, in part, the matter of the visible church. Since they are the matter of the invisible church, as previously proven, none will deny that they are also part of the visible church.

2. A question may arise whether those who profess Christianity, claim regeneration, and profess to love and believe in Christ, but who may lack true regeneration or vital union with Christ, can be considered part of the matter and members of the visible church. To answer this, they are not vital members, but they are members nonetheless and should be regarded as such. The church has always included such individuals, of whom there may be reason to suspect insincerity, yet they are recognized and treated as members by both God and the church,

and outward church privileges should not be denied them. I prove this with the following arguments:

First, a visible profession of Christianity and regeneration is all that we can discern. We may have good hopes that certain individuals truly love God, are regenerated, and are united to Christ. Yet, how often are we mistaken, finding, to our grief, that those of whom we had high hopes make *shipwreck* of what appeared to be faith and a good conscience? As it is written, "They went out from us, but they were not of us; for if they had been of us, they would no doubt have continued with us: but *they went out*, that they might be made manifest that they were not all of us," (1 John 2:19). The church judges based on profession, but only the Lord Christ judges saving grace and union with Him. As Mr. Corbet notes, "Many profess Christianity, or dedication to God in Christ, that are not really, that is, heartily and entirely so dedicated." He adds, "Those who, by such an external profession, are of this society, though but analogically, and as to the external form only, have just right and title to its external privileges, according to their disposedness before them that can discern of things that only appear outwardly." In this way, if men deny them these privileges, they do them wrong.

Second, in the apostles' days, those who made such an outward profession were received into the church and admitted to communion, as is clear beyond dispute in Acts 2:41-42, "Then they that gladly received his word were baptized: and the same day there were added unto them about three thousand souls. And they continued stedfastly in the apostles' doctrine and fellowship, and in breaking of bread, and in prayers." Here, as soon as they professed belief, even within hours of their conversion—that is, professed repentance for their sins and faith in Jesus Christ—they were baptized without delay to *ascertain* the sincerity of their repentance. Soon after, they were admitted to the Lord's Supper, as indicated by "breaking of bread." This was not a singular instance but the apostles' consistent practice, as seen in Acts 8:13, "Then Simon himself believed also: and when he was baptized, he continued with Philip, and wondered, beholding the miracles and signs which were done," and Acts 16:30-31, "And brought them out, and said, Sirs, what must I do to be saved? And they said, Believe on the Lord Jesus Christ, and thou shalt be saved, and thy house."

Objection: Some may argue that the apostles, by immediate inspiration, knew that those they baptized were truly converted and united to Christ by faith.

Answer: The apostles acted as *ministers* of the gospel according to a gospel rule, to be *imitated by others* in later ages. While they desired true conversion in their hearers, they acted upon a visible profession, which was the basis for baptism. Not all whom they baptized were sincere believers, as is evident from examples such as Ananias and Sapphira in Acts 5:1-2, "But a certain man named Ananias, with Sapphira his wife, sold a possession, And kept back part of the price, his wife also being privy to it, and brought a certain part, and laid it at the apostles' feet," and Simon Magus in Acts 8:9-13, "But there was a certain man, called Simon, which beforetime in the same city used sorcery, and bewitched the people of Samaria, giving out that himself was some great one: To whom they all gave heed, from the least to the greatest, saying, This man is the great power of God. And to him they had regard, because that of long time he had bewitched them with sorceries. But when they believed Philip preaching the things concerning the kingdom of God, and the name of Jesus Christ, they were baptized, both men and women. Then Simon himself believed also: and when he was baptized, he continued with Philip, and wondered, beholding the miracles and signs which were done." Many baptized by the apostles or their delegates enjoyed all external church privileges, yet some proved unorthodox in their beliefs or ungodly in their lives. More will be said on this later.

Before leaving the matter of the visible church, we must address the third point promised: to prove that the infants of believing parents are part of the matter of the visible church. This will be the subject of the second chapter.

Chapter 2: Membership

Proving that the infants of believing parents are, in part, the visible matter of the visible church; also showing who is the head, and what is the form and end of the visible church.

Although I have thoroughly addressed this matter elsewhere in my work, *Infant Baptism, God's Ordinance*, Part 1, pages 18–20, and in Part 2, I will now offer further arguments to demonstrate that some infants are visible church members.[2] My argument proceeds as follows:

1. If, by God's merciful appointment, infants were once admitted into the visible church by virtue of the covenant of grace, and if that merciful grant has *never* been repealed or revoked by God, then it is certain that some infants remain members of the visible church. The premise is true: by God's own appointment, some infants were admitted into the visible church by virtue of the covenant of grace, and that privilege has never been repealed. Therefore, it follows that some infants (namely, the infants of believing parents) are still visible church members. This argument involves three points:

---

[2] This work has been republished by Puritan Publications.

1. Some infants were once admitted by God's own appointment into the visible church.

2. They were admitted by virtue of the covenant of grace.

3. This infant church membership has *never* been repealed or revoked.

2. That infants were admitted by God's own appointment into the visible church as visible church members is evident. It is undeniable that among the Jews, infants at eight days old were solemnly admitted into the visible church through circumcision, as commanded in Genesis 17:12, "And he that is eight days old shall be circumcised among you, every man child in your generations, he that is born in the house, or bought with money of any stranger, which is not of thy seed." To demand further proof of this would be as unnecessary as bringing a candle to see the sun.

3. That this infant church membership was by virtue of the covenant of grace is equally certain. In Deuteronomy 29:10–15, we read, "Ye stand this day all of you before the LORD your God; your captains of your tribes, your elders, and your officers, with all the men of Israel, Your little ones, your wives, and

thy stranger that is in thy camp, from the hewer of thy wood unto the drawer of thy water: That thou shouldest enter into covenant with the LORD thy God, and into his oath, which the LORD thy God maketh with thee this day: That he may establish thee to day for a people unto himself, and that he may be unto thee a God, as he hath said unto thee, and as he hath sworn unto thy fathers, to Abraham, to Isaac, and to Jacob. Neither with you only do I make this covenant and this oath; But with him that standeth here with us this day before the LORD our God, and also with him that is not here with us this day." Here, God solemnly renews with both parents and their little ones the covenant made with Abraham in Genesis 17:7, "And I will establish my covenant between me and thee and thy seed after thee in their generations for an everlasting covenant, to be a God unto thee, and to thy seed after thee." Infants, being thus solemnly admitted into the visible church by God Himself through the covenant of grace, were treated as church members. This is shown not only by their circumcision on the eighth day, which was the *seal* of the *covenant of grace* (Genesis 17:12), but also by their being brought to church assemblies, as in

Deuteronomy 29:11 and Deuteronomy 31:10–12, "And Moses commanded them, saying, At the end of every seven years, in the solemnity of the year of release, in the feast of tabernacles, When all Israel is come to appear before the LORD thy God in the place which he shall choose, thou shalt read this law before all Israel in their hearing. Gather the people together, men, and women, and children, and thy stranger that is within thy gates, that they may hear, and that they may learn, and fear the LORD your God, and observe to do all the words of this law."

That this covenant, by which infants were admitted into the visible church by God's appointment, is the covenant of grace is the universal judgment of all sound churches and divines. This could be substantiated with numerous examples. Even Mr. Tombs, one of the most capable among our mistaken brethren who deny infant church membership and baptism, concedes in his *Apology*, page 131, that it was a covenant containing redemption by Christ—a sufficient argument to prove it is the covenant of grace. Those seeking further arguments to confirm that this is the covenant of grace may consult my work, *Infant Baptism, God's Ordinance*, pages 16–17, Part II, where I will also add additional proof in due course.

3. Let us now consider whether this infant church membership was repealed or revoked by Christ in establishing the gospel church.

That infant church membership was never repealed or revoked, I prove as follows:

1. If infants, who were once visible church members, have been cast out and their privileges revoked, such a repeal must be recorded *somewhere* in holy Scripture. If anyone claims it is so recorded, let them show where. But if no such record exists in Scripture stating that infants, once church members, are cast out, then it is beyond all rational contradiction that some infants remain church members. Since no such repeal is recorded, the privilege continues for them.

I have encountered many weak objections from our mistaken brethren, the Anabaptists, but their strongest argument seems to be this: the Jewish church, along with circumcision and the Abrahamic covenant, has been abolished, and the Jews have been cast off, so infant church membership has been repealed.

Answer: The covenant of grace has always *been the same*. It has, indeed, been more clearly revealed over time, but it remains the same covenant. The covenant made with Abraham in Genesis 17:7, "And I will establish my covenant between me and thee and thy seed after thee in their generations for an everlasting covenant, to be a God unto thee, and to thy seed after thee," is the same covenant made with Adam in Genesis 3:15, "And I will put enmity between thee and the woman, and between thy seed and her seed; it shall bruise thy head, and thou shalt bruise his heel." It was merely a clearer expression of that covenant. This same covenant has been the foundation of the church throughout history, with brighter revelations as the time of Christ's appearance drew nearer. In this way, the covenant of grace under the gospel is but a clearer and more radiant expression of the covenant made with Adam and Abraham. The Jews were not all cast off; only *some* were broken off for their unbelief. Believing Jews were not placed on a new foundation but remained in the same covenant. The Gentiles, added to the church, were grafted into the *same stock and root* as the believing Jews, partaking of the same covenant and privileges that the unbelieving Jews lost. This is abundantly clear to any impartial reader, as the apostle states in Romans 11:17, "And if some of the branches be broken off, and thou, being a wild olive tree, wert graffed in among them, and with them partakest of the root and fatness of the olive tree." There could be no clearer proof: as the unbelieving Jews and their children were broken off, the believing Gentiles and their children were grafted into the same stock, standing on the same covenant as the believing Jews.

2. Infant church membership is not repealed, for our Lord Jesus Christ assures us that the gospel church is, in part, composed of such, as in Matthew 19:13–14, "Then were there brought unto him little children, that he should put his hands on them, and pray: and the disciples rebuked them. But Jesus said, Suffer little children, and forbid them not, to come unto me: for of such is the kingdom of heaven." The question arises: for what purpose were these infants brought to Christ? It was not for baptism, as Christ Himself did not baptize, but His disciples did (John 4:2). It is likely they were already baptized. Nor was it for healing, as the disciples knew Christ healed and would not have rebuked them for that. Rather, it was so Christ might *pray over them and bless them*. The disciples, being at that time spiritually immature in many respects, likely shared the same misconception as our mistaken brethren, the Anabaptists, believing that infants were incapable of receiving anything from Christ and that bringing them to Him was futile. But Christ disagreed, commanding that little

children be brought to Him, giving the reason, "for of such is the kingdom of heaven." Here, "the kingdom of heaven" refers to the gospel church in this world, as the phrase is commonly used in Scripture, such as in Matthew 4:17, "From that time Jesus began to preach, and to say, Repent: for the kingdom of heaven is at hand," Matthew 10:7, "And as ye go, preach, saying, The kingdom of heaven is at hand," and Matthew 13:24, 33, 44, 45, 47, where parables describe the kingdom of heaven *as* the gospel church. If "the kingdom of heaven" refers to the gospel church in these and many other passages, then Matthew 19:14 must be understood in the same way. In this way, it is evident that infants are members of the gospel church, just as they were of the Jewish church.

3. That infants are members of the gospel church, I argue from Acts 2:39, where it is written, "For the *promise* is unto you, *and to your children*, and to all that are afar off, even as many as the Lord our God shall call." If this promise is the same as the covenant made with Abraham in Genesis 17:7, "And I will establish my covenant between me and thee and thy seed after thee in their generations for an everlasting

covenant, to be a God unto thee, and to thy seed after thee," and if "children" here corresponds to "seed" there, then the infants of believing Christians are visible church members now, just as the infants of the Jews were then. The premise is true; therefore, the conclusion follows.

4. The promise mentioned in Acts 2:39 is that great promise made to Abraham, for it is a promise of pardon, life, and God's commitment to be their God. It is a promise well known to the Jews, as indicated by the Greek term ἡ ἐπαγγελία (*repromissio*, a repeating of a promise). The definite article ἡ points, as with a finger, to a specific, well-known promise. This promise must be one that circumcision sealed in the past and that baptism now seals, or it would have been meaningless to these awakened Jews. It was the great promise they were most familiar with, offering the greatest comfort in their present distress.

5. By "children" in Acts 2:39, the same is meant as "seed" in Genesis 17:7, these terms being *synonymous*. In this way, the plain meaning of the apostle is this: "Repent, and be baptized every one of you in the name of Jesus Christ for the remission of sins, and ye

shall receive the gift of the Holy Ghost," (Acts 2:38), for the great promise God made to your father Abraham, "I will be a God unto thee, and to thy seed after thee," (Genesis 17:7), remains firm for you and your children. This serves as strong evidence for infant church *membership*. For those desiring a clearer exposition of this text, I refer them to my work, *Infant Baptism, God's Ordinance*, Part II, pages 20–21 and following.

6. That infants are visible church members, I further argue from 1 Corinthians 7:14, "For the unbelieving husband is sanctified by the wife, and the unbelieving wife is sanctified by the husband: else were your children unclean; but now are they holy." The "holiness" here cannot refer to legitimacy of birth nor to true inward sanctification, but to a *federal holiness*—that is, inclusion in the covenant of grace and membership in the visible church. Much more could be said to prove infant church membership, but these arguments suffice.

Though many arguments could be advanced to support infant baptism, for me, this one is *instar omnia* (*equivalent to all others*), an argument so compelling that it decisively settles the matter and against which no solid objection can stand: Those infants who are to be received as visible church members ought to be baptized, and it is a *grievous sin* to deny them this privilege. Baptism is the only rite appointed by Jesus Christ for admitting *visible* church members. Who would dare deny baptism to a visible member of the church? For those seeking further proof of infant baptism, I direct them to my aforementioned books on this subject.

III. Let us now consider the form of the visible church. As previously shown, the form of the invisible church is the union of the church with Christ, its spiritual head, accomplished by the Holy Spirit drawing believers to Christ and faith laying hold of Him. Correspondingly, the form of the visible church consists of a visible profession of Christianity and regeneration, which is necessary for visible church membership among adults. This profession can be understood through two key aspects:

1. God, in His grace, provides the gospel and the means of grace to a people, sending ministers of His Word to offer salvation in the name of Jesus Christ. Through this, they are externally and visibly called and invited to enter into a covenant relationship with God and Christ. This is evident in Matthew 28:19–20, "Go ye therefore, and teach all nations,

baptizing them in the name of the Father, and of the Son, and of the Holy Ghost: Teaching them to observe all things whatsoever I have commanded you: and, lo, I am with you alway, even unto the end of the world. Amen," and Mark 16:15, "And he said unto them, Go ye into all the world, and preach the gospel to every creature." Likewise, 2 Corinthians 5:20 states, "Now then we are ambassadors for Christ, as though God did beseech you by us: we pray you in Christ's stead, be ye reconciled to God." Thus, the *preaching of the gospel* is the divinely appointed means of gathering a visible church.

2. When the gospel is preached and received by a people, God, through His Word, works in them a willingness to enter into His covenant. When a people, either sincerely or at least outwardly, profess Christ, appear willing to receive Him, and believe the great doctrines of the gospel, they are baptized in His name and become God's visible church. Just as the indwelling of the Holy Spirit and saving faith constitute the invisible form, a credible profession of Christianity constitutes the outward form. Therefore, the apostle, guided without error, accepted a profession of faith in Christ as sufficient

for church membership and baptism, without waiting to observe the future obedience of those professing, as seen in Acts 2:41, "Then they that gladly received his word were baptized: and the same day there were added unto them about three thousand souls," and Acts 8:13, "Then Simon himself believed also: and when he was baptized, he continued with Philip, and wondered, beholding the miracles and signs which were done." The apostles would not have done this had they not been directed by the Holy Spirit of God.

IV. The head of the visible church, as with the invisible, is solely Jesus Christ, as affirmed in Colossians 1:18, "And he is the head of the body, the church: who is the beginning, the firstborn from the dead; that in all things he might have the preeminence." Christ is the King and great lawgiver of His church, the chief cornerstone upon which the church is built, as stated in 1 Peter 2:4–5, "To whom coming, as unto a living stone, disallowed indeed of men, but chosen of God, and precious, Ye also, as lively stones, are built up a spiritual house, an holy priesthood, to offer up spiritual sacrifices, acceptable to God by Jesus Christ."

V. The end of the visible church is to worship and glorify God and to be thereby prepared to enjoy Him forever.

Its purposes include holding forth the word of life, preserving the ordinances in their purity, contending earnestly for the faith, honoring and glorifying God through holiness, and ultimately being made blessed in the sweet and perfect enjoyment of God in heaven.

In this way, we have considered the church as visible and invisible, as triumphant in heaven or militant on earth, and as catholic or universal. It now remains to address particular churches.

Chapter 3: Nature of the Church

A Particular Church Described in its nature, 2. In its parts, 3. In its ministry and officers.

Let us consider a particular church in its nature. Since the militant catholic church cannot gather together in one place to worship God, it is distinguished or divided into *particular* churches, or smaller societies. These may be national, provincial, diocesan, or congregational. A national church refers to the inhabitants of one nation or kingdom, living under the same government and jointly professing the Christian faith, such as the church in England, Scotland, Holland, Geneva, or similar regions. Likewise, a provincial or diocesan church may be considered in the same way. However, when the term "church" is used in this sense, it does not mean that all Christians in such a nation or province form one individual congregation under the same church leaders. Rather, it refers to several particular congregations, each under *the rule and oversight* of their own bishop or bishops, associated together by mutual consent. As Mr. Troughton rightly observes, a parochial or congregational church is the only organic church directly and immediately appointed by the Lord Jesus Christ. These congregational churches are the focus of our present consideration.

A particular church may be defined as follows: A particular church is a society of persons professing Christianity and regeneration, living in the same neighborhood so as to conveniently meet together in one place. They are bound by a mutual covenant, first to God and then to one another, to worship God in purity, to perform the mutual duties of church members toward each other, and to walk together in due obedience to all God's ordinances and to the pastor or pastors set over them in the Lord.

Observe the following: a particular church should have no more members than can conveniently meet together in one place, nor more than the church officers can *effectively oversee* in their pastoral *charge*. This ensures that *members* can perform the mutual duties of church membership toward one another. The particular churches described in the New Testament, such as those in Corinth, Ephesus, or Philippi, consisted of members living in the same city, town, or village, enabling them to meet conveniently and maintain personal communion with one another. We find no example in holy Scripture of churches so large or so geographically dispersed that the minister could not oversee all the members or that the members could not frequently meet for personal communion.

The *members* of a particular church are bound by a *covenant* to God and to one another. To God, as the apostle suggests in 1 Corinthians 8:5, "And this they did, not as we hoped, but first gave their own selves to the Lord, and unto us by the will of God," (1 Corinthians 8:5). In baptism, we seal our commitment to the covenant of grace, and in riper years, when admitted to the Lord's Supper, we renew our baptismal engagement to be the Lord's forever. Likewise, *members covenant with one another* to walk together in all God's ordinances and to fulfill the mutual duties of church members, as also implied in 2 Corinthians 8:5, "And this they did, not as we hoped, but first gave their own selves to the Lord, and unto us by the will of God," to be governed according to gospel order. It should also be noted that all particular churches possess *an inherent authority* to form themselves and govern themselves according to the laws of Christ.

Particular churches, as parts and members of the universal catholic militant church on earth, vary in their purity depending on the time and place in which they exist. Since the church exists in a fallen world, which is marked by corruption, and since even the best of God's children, including ministers and church rulers, bear the remnants of ignorance, pride, and other corruptions, the church remains in a state of great imperfection. Moreover, some individuals who lack a vital union with Christ and are not members of the invisible church may intrude into the visible church for unworthy motives, significantly hindering its reformation. Consequently, particular churches differ in their degree of purity and reformation, some being far more faithful to the gospel than others.

This may be compared to a town or city, where some inhabitants are healthy, others suffer from minor ailments that do not prevent them from their duties, and still others are gravely ill, near death. Similarly, in the visible church, some particular churches are far more sound and pure, adhering *closely* to the rules of the gospel in both doctrine and evangelical discipline. Yet even in the purest and most reformed churches, there remains, and will remain in this world, some imperfection. This is evident even in the purest churches recorded in the New Testament, planted by the apostles themselves.

Consider the renowned church of Corinth, which abounded in spiritual gifts to such an extent that, when they gathered, there was scarcely room to exercise them all, as described in 1 Corinthians 14:26, "How is it then, brethren?

when ye come together, every one of you hath a psalm, hath a doctrine, hath a tongue, hath a revelation, hath an interpretation. Let all things be done unto edifying." The members of this church were filled with the Spirit in an extraordinary manner, yet *much was amiss*. There were divisions and factions, with some exalting one minister above another, as noted in 1 Corinthians 1:12, "Now this I say, that every one of you saith, I am of Paul; and I of Apollos; and I of Cephas; and I of Christ," which caused great contentions. Some in the church even denied the resurrection of the dead, as in 1 Corinthians 15:12, "Now if Christ be preached that he rose from the dead, how say some among you that there is no resurrection of the dead?" There were also significant disorders in their approach to the Lord's Table, as mentioned in 1 Corinthians 11:20–21, "When ye come together therefore into one place, this is not to eat the Lord's supper. For in eating every one taketh before other his own supper: and one is hungry, and another is drunken."

Likewise, imperfections were found in other notable churches, such as those in Ephesus, Galatia, Smyrna, Pergamos, and others. Some churches were even more corrupt, such as those in Sardis and Laodicea, as described in Revelation 3:1–3, "And unto the angel of the church in

Sardis write; These things saith he that hath the seven Spirits of God, and the seven stars; I know thy works, that thou hast a name that thou livest, and art dead. Be watchful, and strengthen the things which remain, that are ready to die: for I have not found thy works perfect before God. Remember therefore how thou hast received and heard, and hold fast, and repent," and Revelation 3:16–20, "So then because thou art lukewarm, and neither cold nor hot, I will spue thee out of my mouth. Because thou sayest, I am rich, and increased with goods, and have need of nothing; and knowest not that thou art wretched, and miserable, and poor, and blind, and naked: I counsel thee to buy of me gold tried in the fire, that thou mayest be rich; and white raiment, that thou mayest be clothed, and that the shame of thy nakedness do not appear; and anoint thine eyes with eyesalve, that thou mayest see. As many as I love, I rebuke and chasten: be zealous therefore, and repent. Behold, I stand at the door, and knock: if any man hear my voice, and open the door, I will come in to him, and will sup with him, and he with me." From this, I would draw one or two inferences.

1. From the foregoing, it is clear that a particular church may have many faults and yet remain a true church of Christ. Here, I will cite the words of the

learned French Protestant, Lord Plessis Mornay, who writes in his *Treatise of the Church*, page 31: "There are erring churches, which err either heretically or schismatically, either in faith or in charity, contrary to the right rule of Christ; and yet, for all this, both the one and the other are truly churches, that is, assemblies that make profession of Christ, but they are not pure churches, not serving God in purity. Just as a lying person is truly a man, though not a truthful man, or a person under some disease is a man, though not a sound and healthy man." In this way, we should not hastily conclude that churches are not churches simply because they have many imperfections.

2. When separating from any church, we must not do so in a way that breaks Christian charity. We may, and indeed must, separate from the sins and corruptions of a church, having no fellowship with the unfruitful works of darkness, as it is written, "And have no fellowship with the unfruitful works of darkness, but rather reprove them," (Ephesians 5:11). However, we should not rashly or lightly declare a people to be no church because of some remaining corruptions among them. Instead, we

must strive to maintain the unity of the Spirit in the bond of peace, separating from them only insofar as they *depart from Christ*, while still holding communion with them in all lawful things, as urged in Ephesians 4:3, "Endeavouring to keep the unity of the Spirit in the bond of peace," (Ephesians 4:3).

Objection: Suppose a church makes things the terms of her communion that are either clearly sinful or doubtful and imposes them on me, such that if I do not conform, I am suspended, excommunicated, or cut off from the communion of that church.

Answer: In such a case, I do not willfully separate myself from them. I would gladly maintain communion with them in all lawful things and conform as far as God's Word and my conscience allow. However, if they establish laws and canons requiring a degree of conformity that God's Word and my conscience condemn as sinful, and if, for refusing to comply, I am deprived, suspended, or excommunicated, thereby denied communion, it is my duty to worship God elsewhere. In doing so, I am neither a schismatic nor guilty of any breach of charity, whether I, as a minister, preach or, as a private Christian, join another congregation for Christian communion where such requirements are *not* imposed. The apostle instructs, "Now I beseech you, brethren, mark them which cause divisions and offences contrary to the doctrine which ye have learned; and avoid them," (Romans 16:17). In this way, those who impose *unwarranted terms of church communion*, requiring as necessary for church unity things that God's Word disallows, and who exclude me for not complying, are the true cause of the schism. A learned gentleman, a justice of the peace who lived and died in the communion of the Church of England, Mr. Polehill of Burwash, in his printed discourse on schism, so thoroughly clears Protestant dissenters from the charge of this sin that I need say no more. I refer the reader to his small treatise, particularly the seventh chapter, for further satisfaction on this matter.

3. Although I may be forced, by unwarranted terms of communion, to join another congregation, I dare not declare the church from which I was driven to be no church, nor call the church to which I am now united a distinct or separate church, except as it is a part or member of the universal or catholic church. On this basis, I am still willing to maintain communion with other churches, even those less pure or less reformed, provided they hold to the foundation, so long as I can do so without approving or consenting to their corruptions.

Chapter 3: Nature of the Church

II. Next, let us consider a particular church in its parts. Every particular church may be understood as consisting of two parts, as represented in Scripture in Acts 20:28, "Take heed therefore unto yourselves, and to all the flock, over the which the Holy Ghost hath made you overseers, to feed the church of God, which he hath purchased with his own blood." Here, ministers are called ἐπισκόπους (*episkopous*, bishops or overseers in our translation), while the rest of the church, distinct from its officers, is called ποιμνίον (*poimnion*, a little flock). Thus, the two parts of the church are:

1. The overseers, or ministers, who are the rulers of this flock or church of God.
2. The flock, distinct from its officers, who are to be overseen, fed, ruled, and governed according to God's Word.
3. I begin with the first, namely, the church's officers. These are individuals whom God has *lawfully called*, and whose ministry He uses in the gathering and governing of the church. They are divided into two categories: extraordinary and ordinary.
4. Extraordinary ministers are those whom God raised up on special occasions, either to establish a new government in the church or to restore the old

government when it had decayed. Such ministers always possess extraordinary gifts, such as prophecy, tongues, and miracles. Examples include the prophets of the Old Testament, who were directly called and sent by God, as well as John the Baptist, Jesus Christ, and the apostles in the New Testament. *These* extraordinary ministers, along with their extraordinary gifts, continued, as long as God pleased and the church's needs required. However, such extraordinary callings and miraculous gifts *have now entirely ceased*, for no one is now called or gifted in this manner for the work of the ministry.

5. Ordinary ministers are those with ordinary gifts and an ordinary *calling, appointed* to continue in the church until the end of the world. These ordinary church officers are of two sorts:

6. A lower and inferior sort of officer, whose proper work is to collect and distribute alms or other provisions made by the church for the poor. Though this is an inferior office, as the apostle terms it, "to serve tables" in Acts 6:2, "Then the twelve called the multitude of the disciples unto them, and said, It is not reason that we should leave the word of God,

and serve tables," the power to ordain these officers does not rest *with the people*. The people may choose suitable persons, as in Acts 6:3–5, "Wherefore, brethren, look ye out among you seven men of honest report, full of the Holy Ghost and wisdom, whom we may appoint over this business. But we will give ourselves continually to prayer, and to the ministry of the word. And the saying pleased the whole multitude: and they chose Stephen, a man full of faith and of the Holy Ghost, and Philip, and Prochorus, and Nicanor, and Timon, and Parmenas, and Nicolas a proselyte of Antioch." However, the *apostles ordained them* by fasting, prayer, and the laying on of hands, as in Acts 6:6, "Whom they set before the apostles: and when they had prayed, they laid their hands on them."

7. A higher and more noble order of church officers, whose primary work consists in prayer and the ministry of the Word, as the apostle states in Acts 6:4, "But we will give ourselves continually to prayer, and to the ministry of the word." These church officers are called ἐπισκόπους (*episkopous*, bishops or overseers) in Acts 20:28, "Take heed therefore unto yourselves, and to all the flock, over the which the

Holy Ghost hath made you overseers, to feed the church of God, which he hath purchased with his own blood," and πρεσβυτέρους (*presbuterous*, presbyters or elders) in Acts 20:17, "And from Miletus he sent to Ephesus, and called the elders of the church," (Acts 20:17). They are also described as pastors and teachers in Ephesians 4:11, "And he gave some, apostles; and some, prophets; and some, evangelists; and some, pastors and teachers," (Ephesians 4:11), likely two names for the same office. In describing these church officers, I will address five questions:

I. Are Scripture bishops, presbyters, elders, and pastors distinct offices in the church, or are they different names for the same office?

II. Is the ministry, under the gospel, a standing ordinance, with ministers set apart from others for gospel work?

III. May a mere layman, gifted and desired by a church, ordinarily *preach* and *administer* the sacraments?

IV. Should the ordination of persons to minister in the church be performed with fasting, prayer, and the laying on of hands, or not?

Chapter 3: Nature of the Church

V. Where is the ordaining power lodged by Jesus Christ—in a diocesan bishop, in the elders or presbyters (all pastors of the church), or in the body of the people, that is, the graver members of a particular church?

I. Are Scripture bishops, presbyters, or elders distinct officers in the church, or are they different names for the same kind of church officer?

It is abundantly clear that in the New Testament, a bishop and a presbyter or elder are merely different names for the same church officer, as evidenced by the following:

1. In Acts 20:17, Paul sent to Ephesus for the πρεσβυτέρους (*presbuterous*, elders or presbyters), as it is written, "And from Miletus he sent to Ephesus, and called the elders of the church," (Acts 20:17). These same individuals are called ἐπισκόπους (*episkopous*, bishops or overseers) in Acts 20:28, "Take heed therefore unto yourselves, and to all the flock, over the which the Holy Ghost hath made you overseers, to feed the church of God, which he hath purchased with his own blood." In this way, those termed elders in verse 17 are called bishops in verse 28.
2. It is clear from Philippians 1:1, "Paul and Timotheus, the servants of Jesus Christ, to all the saints in Christ

Jesus which are at Philippi, with the bishops and deacons." Here, the church has only two sorts of officers: bishops and deacons. Deacons were responsible for caring for the poor, so the term "bishops" must refer to the same officers called elders in Acts 20:17. In the Syriac version, this is rendered as presbyters and ministers, showing that "bishop" and "presbyter" are used *interchangeably* for the same church officer. Similarly, in 1 Timothy 3:1, the apostle speaks of the office of a bishop, "This is a true saying, If a man desire the office of a bishop, he desireth a good work," without mentioning any other church office until he addresses deacons in verse 12, "Let the deacons be the husbands of one wife, ruling their children and their own houses well," (1 Timothy 3:12). This indicates that the apostle recognized *no other office* to be ordained in the church, and thus "bishops" must refer to the same officers previously called presbyters or elders.

3. This is further supported by learned Protestant divines. Mr. Corbet, in his *Remains*, page 111, gathers many testimonies from antiquity to prove that a bishop and a presbyter *are the same*. Likewise, the learned Gualtherus Zanchius states that presbyters

and bishops are, by divine right, both ministering in the same office and by virtue of the same authority. Most English Protestant divines share this view.

Question II. Is the ministry, under the gospel, a standing ordinance, with ministers set apart from others for gospel work?

I affirm this and prove it with the following arguments:

Argument 1. The ministry is a standing ordinance, for from the beginning of the world, *God has set apart* a certain order of men for the ministry. Under the law, not everyone could be a priest; the priesthood initially belonged to the firstborn, as in Genesis 25:31, "And Jacob said, Sell me this day thy birthright." Later, it was conferred upon the Levites, as in Numbers 3:15–17, "Number the children of Levi after the house of their fathers, by their families: every male from a month old and upward shalt thou number them. And Moses numbered them according to the word of the LORD, as he was commanded. And these were the sons of Levi by their names; Gershon, and Kohath, and Merari," (Numbers 3:15–17). The priesthood rested in the tribe of Levi, ordained and set apart *by God* to serve in the tabernacle, and this continued until the coming of Christ. Those who invaded this office were severely punished by God, as seen in the dreadful example of Numbers 16:2–3, "And they rose up before Moses, with certain of the children of Israel, two hundred and fifty princes of the assembly, famous in the congregation, men of renown: And they gathered themselves together against Moses and against Aaron, and said unto them, Ye take too much upon you, seeing all the congregation are holy, every one of them, and the LORD is among them: wherefore then lift ye up yourselves above the congregation of the LORD?" The priesthood was, by God's appointment, fixed in Aaron and his sons, but Korah and his company accused Moses and Aaron of pride and usurpation, claiming that the entire congregation was a kingdom of priests *with equal right to minister*. The controversy was whether only Aaron and his sons were priests or whether the whole congregation had the same right. God resolved this dispute decisively, ordering Aaron and his sons on one side and Korah and his company on the other to appear before the Lord with their censers, as in Numbers 16:5–7, 9–10, 16–18. The earth opened and swallowed Korah and his company, along with their wives, children, and goods, as described in Numbers 16:31–33, "And it came to pass, as he had made an end of speaking all these words, that the ground clave asunder that was under them: And the earth opened her mouth, and swallowed them up, and their houses, and all the men that appertained unto Korah, and all their goods. They, and all that appertained to them, went down alive into the pit, and the earth closed upon them: and they perished from among the congregation." This serves as a terrible warning against *those who invade the ministry.*

Though Christ abolished the Aaronic priesthood, He established the gospel ministry in its place, to continue until the end of the world. Christ appointed His twelve apostles and sent them, along with the seventy disciples, to preach, as in Luke 9:1-2, "Then he called his twelve disciples together, and gave them power and authority over all devils, and to cure diseases. And he sent them to preach the kingdom of God, and to heal the sick." These, by fasting, prayer, and the laying on of hands, ordained and sent forth others, as evident in Acts 1:24-25, "And they prayed, and said, Thou, Lord, which knowest the hearts of all men, shew whether of these two thou hast chosen, That he may take part of this ministry and apostleship, from which Judas by transgression fell, that he might go to his own place," Acts 6:6, "Whom they set before the apostles: and when they had prayed, they laid their hands on them," and Acts 14:23, "And when they had ordained them elders in every church, and had prayed with fasting, they commended them to the Lord, on whom they believed." This practice continued in the primitive church and was *undisputed* until the last century, when innovators in Germany, such as Servetus, Knipperdoling, and John of Leiden, along with the Socinians, began to challenge it. From these, those in England who deny or invade the ministry have borrowed their arguments.

Argument 2. An ordinance to which many precious promises are made must continue until those promises are fulfilled. Many promises are made to ministers and the gospel ministry, and these will not be fully fulfilled until the end of the world; therefore, the gospel ministry must continue. Long before Christ's coming, God promised the gospel church a distinct order of ministers, as in Isaiah 52:7–8, "How beautiful upon the mountains are the feet of him that bringeth good tidings, that publisheth peace; that bringeth good tidings of good, that publisheth salvation; that saith unto Zion, Thy God reigneth! Thy watchmen shall lift up the voice; with the voice together shall they sing: for they shall see eye to eye, when the LORD shall bring again Zion." That this refers to more than deliverance from Babylon and promises a gospel ministry is clear from Romans 10:14–17, "How then shall they call on him in whom they have not believed? and how shall they believe in him of whom they have not heard? and how shall they hear without a preacher? And how shall they preach, except they be sent? as it is written, How beautiful are the feet of them that preach the gospel of peace, and bring glad tidings of good things! But they have not all obeyed the gospel. For Esaias saith, Lord, who hath believed our report? So then faith cometh by hearing, and hearing by the word of God." Further, Isaiah 62:6–7 states, "I have set watchmen upon thy walls, O Jerusalem, which shall never hold their peace day nor night: ye that make mention of the LORD, keep not silence, And give him no rest, till he establish, and till he make Jerusalem a praise in the earth," and Jeremiah 3:15, "And I will give you pastors according to mine heart, which shall feed you with knowledge and understanding." And Jeremiah 23:4, "And I will set up shepherds over them which shall feed them: and they shall fear no more, nor be dismayed, neither shall they be lacking, saith the LORD." These, and many other passages, are promises of a *gospel ministry*, as most, if not all, orthodox divines interpret them. Additionally, Matthew 28:20 promises, "Teaching them to observe all things whatsoever I have commanded you: and, lo, I am with you alway, even unto the end of the world. Amen."

Argument 3. If the ministry was appointed by Christ for the perfecting of the saints, it must continue until the saints are perfected, which will not occur until all are gathered into heaven. This is true, as stated in Ephesians 4:11–12, "And he gave some, apostles; and some, prophets; and some, evangelists; and some, pastors and teachers; For the perfecting of the saints, for the work of the ministry, for the edifying of the body of Christ."

Argument 4. If Jesus Christ in the gospel made provision for a gospel ministry, then the gospel ministry is *God's ordinance*. This is true, as in Galatians 6:6, "Let him that is taught in the word communicate unto him that teacheth in all good things," and 1 Corinthians 9:14, "Even so hath the Lord ordained that they which preach the gospel should live of the gospel."

Argument 5. If the gospel calls the ministry *an office*, it is certainly an office. The gospel does so, as in 1 Timothy 3:1, "This is a true saying, If a man desire the office of a bishop, he desireth a good work," identifying ministers as *officers* of Jesus Christ.

Question III. May a mere layman or private Christian, who has gifts and is desired by a church or group of Christians to exercise them, ordinarily preach and administer the sacraments?

To avoid misunderstanding, this question does not concern:

1. Those trained and intended for the ministry who preach occasionally before ordination to demonstrate their ability (*ad probandam facultatem*).
2. What may be done where no ministry is available.
3. What persons extraordinarily called, such as prophets or apostles, may do.
4. What private Christians may and ought to do in their families.
5. Whether Christians may, outside of public worship times on the Lord's Day or other days, meet to pray, sing psalms, repeat sermons, or share their experiences with one another.

These activities are acknowledged as the clear *duty of Christians*. The question is whether it is lawful for private Christians, however gifted and desired, to exercise those gifts in a ministerial capacity by taking a text, making observations, preaching, or administering the sacraments in public church assemblies.

The answer is that it is sinful and unlawful for any private Christian, except as allowed above, no matter how gifted or desired, in a well-ordered church, to undertake the preaching of the Word or the administration of the sacraments.

This I prove with the following arguments:

Argument 1. Those who undertake to administer any gospel ordinance without a precept, promise, or example in God's Word sin in so doing. For a mere private Christian (except as previously noted) to administer any gospel ordinance peculiar to the ministry, such as preaching or the sacraments, is to act *without any promise, precept, or approved example in all of God's Word*. Therefore, such a person sins greatly in doing so.

This is abundantly clear in the New Testament, which teaches that gospel precepts require, and gospel examples demonstrate, that those who preach the gospel must not only have grace and abilities and be desired to exercise them but must also be solemnly set apart for the work. This is evident in Titus 1:5, "For this cause left I thee in Crete, that thou shouldest set in order the things that are wanting, and ordain elders in every city, as I had appointed thee." By "elders" here, the text does not refer to gifted brethren in general but to bishops and presbyters, as indicated in Titus 1:6–9. These must be *ordained*, as I will show shortly.

Another command is found in 1 Timothy 5:22, "Lay hands suddenly on no man, neither be partaker of other men's sins: keep thyself pure." This means to ordain ministers to administer gospel ordinances with great deliberation, ensuring that unfit persons are not appointed to this office. This is clear from the context in 1 Timothy 5:17–21, "Let the elders that rule well be counted worthy of double honour, especially they who labour in the word and doctrine. For the scripture saith, Thou shalt not muzzle the ox that treadeth out the corn. And, The labourer is worthy of his reward. Against an elder receive not an accusation, but before two or three witnesses. Them that sin rebuke before all, that others also may fear. I charge thee before God, and the Lord Jesus Christ, and the elect angels, that thou observe these things without preferring one before another, doing nothing by partiality."

Another precept is in Acts 13:2–3, "As they ministered to the Lord, and fasted, the Holy Ghost said, Separate me Barnabas and Saul for the work whereunto I have called them. And when they had fasted and prayed, and laid their hands on them, they sent them away." It is noteworthy that, although Paul and Barnabas were extraordinarily called to the ministry and possessed miraculous gifts, God *commanded* them to be *solemnly set apart* for the work by fasting, prayer, and the laying on of hands. In this way, Scripture precepts require those who preach to be *solemnly set apart*. Likewise, gospel examples show that those sent to preach were solemnly ordained, and *none* went out without such *ordination*. The apostles themselves, besides their fitness for the work, received a *commission* from Jesus Christ, as in Matthew 28:19-20, "Go ye therefore, and teach all nations, baptizing them in the name of the Father, and of the Son, and of the Holy Ghost: Teaching them to observe all things whatsoever I have commanded you: and, lo, I am with you alway, even unto the end of the world. Amen." In Acts 6:6, men full of the Holy Ghost were ordained, "Whom they set before the apostles: and when they had prayed, they laid their hands on them." This was the practice in *all* churches; none were sent out until solemnly set apart, as seen in Acts 20:17, 28 and 1 Timothy 5:17.

Argument 2. For anyone to *assume* an act of office without being an officer is *sinful*. For even if "gifted" brethren undertake preaching or similar acts on their own, it is still an *act of office*; therefore, it is sinful. Preaching the gospel is an act of office proper to ministers, as is clear from 1 Timothy 5:17, "Let the elders that rule well be counted worthy of double honour, especially they who labour in the word and doctrine," Titus 1:5, 9, Acts 20:17, 28, 1 Corinthians 4:1, "Let a man so account of us, as of the ministers of Christ, and stewards of the mysteries of God," (1 Corinthians 4:1), 1 Timothy 2:7, "Whereunto I am ordained a preacher, and an apostle, (I speak the truth in Christ, and lie not;) a teacher of the Gentiles in faith and verity," (1 Timothy 2:7), and 2 Timothy 2:11, "It is a faithful saying: For if we be dead with him, we shall also live with him." Even in civil affairs, it is sinful for a private person to assume the duties of a constable, recorder, mayor, justice of the peace, or judge—how much more so in matters of religion? Preaching the gospel is the primary and chief part of *a minister's office*, the first duty in the commission, as in Matthew 28:20, "Teaching them to observe all things whatsoever I have commanded you: and, lo, I am with you alway, even unto the end of the world. Amen." Paul considered preaching his great work, as in 1 Corinthians 1:17, "For Christ sent me not to baptize, but to preach the gospel: not with wisdom of words, lest the cross of Christ should be made of none effect," and 2 Timothy 4:2, "Preach the word; be instant in season, out of season; reprove, rebuke, exhort with all longsuffering and doctrine."

Argument 3. If God was angry under the law with those who usurped the priestly office, then God, being unchanging, will be angry in the days of the gospel with those who usurp the ministerial office. God was indeed angry with such under the law; therefore, He will be angry with those who do so in the gospel era. The major premise is clear from Hebrews 13:8, "Jesus Christ the same yesterday, and to day, and for ever." The minor premise is proven by:

1. The example of Uzzah in 2 Samuel 6:6–8, "And when they came to Nachon's threshingfloor, Uzzah put forth his hand to the ark of God, and took hold of it; for the oxen shook it. And the anger of the LORD was kindled against Uzzah; and God smote him there for his error; and there he died by the ark of God. And David was displeased, because the LORD had made a breach upon Uzzah: and he called the name of the place Perezuzzah to this day." Uzzah died for touching the ark, which only priests were permitted to handle, as in Numbers 4:16, "And to the office of Eleazar the son of Aaron the priest pertaineth the oil for the light, and the sweet incense, and the daily meat offering, and the anointing oil, and the oversight of all the tabernacle, and of all that therein is, in the sanctuary, and in the vessels thereof." Uzzah's intention was good—he sought to prevent the ark from falling—but good intentions cannot justify irregular actions. Oh, that those who thrust themselves into the ministry would remember Uzzah! Their intentions may be good, but God judged him for it.

Chapter 3: Nature of the Church

2. The example of King Uzziah in 2 Chronicles 26:16–20, "But when he was strong, his heart was lifted up to his destruction: for he transgressed against the LORD his God, and went into the temple of the LORD to burn incense upon the altar of incense... And they withstood Uzziah the king, and said unto him, It appertaineth not unto thee, Uzziah, to burn incense unto the LORD, but to the priests the sons of Aaron, that are consecrated to burn incense: go out of the sanctuary; for thou hast trespassed; neither shall it be for thine honour from the LORD God... And Uzziah was wroth... and while he was wroth with the priests, the leprosy even rose up in his forehead before the priests in the house of the LORD, from beside the incense altar. And Azariah the chief priest, and all the priests, looked upon him, and, behold, he was leprous in his forehead, and they thrust him out from thence; yea, himself hasted also to go out, because the LORD had smitten him." Uzziah presumed to burn incense, a task reserved for priests, and the Lord struck him with leprosy.

3. Most notably, the example of God's remarkable judgment on Korah, Dathan, and Abiram in Numbers 16:1–4, 39, "Now Korah, the son of Izhar,

the son of Kohath, the son of Levi, and Dathan and Abiram, the sons of Eliab, and On, the son of Peleth, sons of Reuben, took men: And they rose up before Moses, with certain of the children of Israel, two hundred and fifty princes of the assembly, famous in the congregation, men of renown: And they gathered themselves together against Moses and against Aaron, and said unto them, Ye take too much upon you, seeing all the congregation are holy, every one of them, and the LORD is among them: wherefore then lift ye up yourselves above the congregation of the LORD? And when Moses heard it, he fell upon his face." These men thrust themselves into the priestly office, claiming, as in verse 3, that all the congregation was holy and *could* offer sacrifice, preach, and pray as well as Aaron. This is the very controversy today: some claim that anyone with gifts may preach. But God's dreadful judgment on Korah and his company, who sought to level both magistracy and ministry, should make bold invaders tremble. The Lord decided the controversy in an awe-inspiring manner, as in Numbers 16:31–33.

Argument 4. If none may preach except those who are sent, then not every gifted person may preach. None may preach except those who are sent, as proven in Romans 10:15, "And how shall they preach, except they be *sent?* as it is written, How beautiful are the feet of them that preach the gospel of peace, and bring glad tidings of good things!" All who preach authoritatively from Christ must be sent either directly by God or Christ, proving their sending with miracles, or mediately by men appointed by Christ to separate, set apart, and *ordain* them for this work. Without such sending, they *cannot preach duly, profitably, or with Christ's authority*. Some run before they are sent, as in Jeremiah 23:21, "I have not sent these prophets, yet they ran: I have not spoken to them, yet they prophesied."

Objection: Gifting is sending.

Answer: I deny this. Gifts are distinct from sending. Many thousands are gifted but *not* sent to preach. Paul and Barnabas had exceptional gifts, yet they were *ordained*, as in Acts 13:1–3, "Now there were in the church that was at Antioch certain prophets and teachers; as Barnabas, and Simeon that was called Niger, and Lucius of Cyrene, and Manaen, which had been brought up with Herod the tetrarch, and Saul. As they ministered to the Lord, and fasted, the Holy Ghost said, Separate me Barnabas and Saul for the work whereunto I have called them. And when they had fasted and prayed, and laid their hands on them, they sent them away." In Matthew 10:1, Christ gifted the apostles, "And when he had called unto him his twelve disciples, he gave them power against unclean spirits, to cast them out, and to heal all manner of sickness and all manner of disease," but also sent them, as in Matthew 10:5, "These twelve Jesus sent forth, and commanded them, saying, Go not into the way of the Gentiles, and into any city of the Samaritans enter ye not."

Argument 5. If all who have gifts may preach, then all who have gifts may baptize, for none may preach who may not baptize; the commission includes both, as in Matthew 28:19, "Go ye therefore, and teach all nations, baptizing them in the name of the Father, and of the Son, and of the Holy Ghost." Preaching is the greater work, baptizing the lesser; thus, one who may do the greater may certainly do the lesser, as in 1 Corinthians 1:17, "For Christ sent me not to baptize, but to preach the gospel: not with wisdom of words, lest the cross of Christ should be made of none effect," meaning comparatively less to baptize than to preach. If a layman has *no commission* to baptize, he has *none* to preach. Few laymen claim authority to baptize.

Argument 6. If none may preach except those who are ordained, then not everyone with gifts may preach. Only those ordained may preach, as clear from Acts 13:3, Acts

15:22, "Then pleased it the apostles and elders, with the whole church, to send chosen men of their own company to Antioch with Paul and Barnabas; namely, Judas surnamed Barsabas, and Silas, chief men among the brethren," and Acts 14:23, "And when they had ordained them elders in every church, and had prayed with fasting, they commended them to the Lord, on whom they believed." More on this will follow.

Argument 7. That which arises from pride or self-conceitedness within us, or from heretical and schismatical disturbers of the church without, cannot be of God, for *qualis causa, talis effectus* (as is the cause, so is the effect). One person invading another's place and office stems from *pride*, as is evident. If I were to intrude into the king's privy council, a judge's seat, or the role of a constable or justice of the peace, it would clearly be rooted in pride. Likewise, the notion that all with gifts may preach was first promoted by Socinians, Arminians, Quakers, Anabaptists, and similar groups in the last century in Germany and elsewhere, making it a *sinful and dangerous practice*. This origin is evident from their own writings and the histories recorded by reformed divines of Germany.

Argument 8. That which contradicts the principles and practices of all reformed churches in every age and place must be highly sinful. The practice of laymen preaching is such, as evidenced by the condemnation of this practice by all ancient fathers and learned divines, including Calvin, Luther, Oecolampadius, Bucer, Chemnitius, Poole, Hammond, Perkins, Burgess, Wolds, Scudder, and countless others, as well as the canons and decrees of councils and the confessions of famous reformed churches in Piedmont, France, Geneva, Helvetia, Scotland, England, and elsewhere. All, as with one voice, *condemn lay preachers as not sent by God.*

Objections Answered:

Error always has something to say for itself, and so do our mistaken brethren. They raise the following objections:

Objection 1. The Lord commends Abraham for teaching his family, as in Genesis 18:19, "For I know him, that he will command his children and his household after him, and they shall keep the way of the LORD, to do justice and judgment; that the LORD may bring upon Abraham that which he hath spoken of him." Therefore, private people may preach.

Answer: This is a *non sequitur*. That Abraham taught his family *does not mean laymen may preach*. It is the duty of every Christian with a family to instruct them in the fear of

God, but this does not imply they may preach publicly. Even if Abraham preached publicly, it does not aid the objectors, for Abraham was a prophet, as in Genesis 20:7, "Now therefore restore the man his wife; for he is a prophet, and he shall pray for thee, and thou shalt live."

Objection 2. Eldad and Medad prophesied, and Moses wished that all the Lord's people were prophets, as in Numbers 11:25-29, "And the LORD came down in a cloud, and spake unto him, and took of the spirit that was upon him, and gave it unto the seventy elders: and it came to pass, that, when the spirit rested upon them, they prophesied, and did not cease... And Joshua the son of Nun, the servant of Moses, one of his young men, answered and said, My lord Moses, forbid them. And Moses said unto him, Enviest thou for my sake? would God that all the LORD'S people were prophets, and that the LORD would put his spirit upon them!" Therefore, we may preach.

Answer: You err, not knowing the Scriptures. The seventy elders, including Eldad and Medad, were extraordinarily called and miraculously gifted, which you are not. Their prophesying was a spirit of *government*, by which God convinced the congregation of Israel that He had chosen these to assist Moses in governance. It is a far-fetched inference to conclude that because God chose seventy elders to assist Moses, anyone with gifts may preach.

Objection 3. It is said in 2 Chronicles 17:7–9, compared with 2 Chronicles 19:6–8, that Jehoshaphat and Hezekiah sent judges and priests to teach the people. Therefore, those not in office may preach.

Answer: This is flawed logic. That judges or others employed by the king to reform the kingdom went from city to city teaching the people about the law does not mean gifted men not in office may preach. Do not our kings instruct judges, and do not judges at every assize give a charge to those present, especially magistrates, often addressing religion? Would it not be absurd to argue, "I may preach because the judge speaks of religion"? Moreover, the civil laws governing the Jewish commonwealth were the holy Scriptures, so reforming the commonwealth required expounding the divine law. Yet, we have no assurance this was done otherwise than by commanding the priests and Levites who accompanied them to perform their duties in preaching and expounding the Scriptures.

Objection 4. Elisha was called from the plow, as in 1 Kings 19:19, "So he departed thence, and found Elisha the son of Shaphat, who was plowing with twelve yoke of oxen before him, and he with the twelfth: and Elijah passed by him, and cast his mantle upon him," and Amos from the herds, as in Amos 7:14–15, "Then answered Amos, and said to Amaziah, I was no prophet, neither was I a prophet's son; but I was an herdman, and a gatherer of sycomore fruit: And the LORD took me as I followed the flock, and the LORD said unto me, Go, prophesy unto my people Israel." Therefore, we may preach.

Answer: Elisha and Amos were miraculously called and qualified. When Amos was forbidden to preach, he did not plead his gifts but his *commission*, as in Amos 7:15.

Objection 5. The apostles were ordinary men, not formally educated scholars, yet they preached, so we may preach.

Answer: Jesus miraculously equipped them with gifts, including the gift of miracles, and gave them a commission, as in Matthew 10:1, 5, "And when he had called unto him his twelve disciples, he gave them power against unclean spirits, to cast them out, and to heal all manner of sickness and all manner of disease... These twelve Jesus sent forth, and commanded them, saying, Go not into the way of the Gentiles, and into any city of the Samaritans enter ye not." Can you prove Christ has done the same for you? If so, we will acknowledge you.

Objection 6. The scribes and Pharisees were not always in office, yet they taught, so we may teach.

Answer: I deny this. They were either priests and Levites, as in John 1:19, 24, "And this is the record of John, when the Jews sent priests and Levites from Jerusalem to ask him, Who art thou?... And they which were sent were of the Pharisees," or prophets, and thus could be from any tribe.

Objection 7. Stephen, being a deacon and not a pastor, *preached*, so we may preach.

Answer: Stephen was an *ordained church officer*. What he said was not a sermon but an apology for himself when accused of blasphemy, as the martyrs did, as in Acts 7. This proves nothing for *lay preaching*.

Objection 8. In Acts 8:4, "Therefore they that were scattered abroad went every where preaching the word," so laymen may preach.

Answer: In persecutions, the rage of enemies falls first and hardest on the ministry. There were many ordained preachers besides the apostles. It is unlikely that the apostles and other ordained ministers remained peacefully in Jerusalem while private Christians were banished. Rather, it seems that ministers and those set apart to preach were driven away and preached everywhere. Even if some were not officers before, they were made so then, for the hand of the Lord was upon them, as in Acts 11:21, "And the hand of the Lord was with them: and a great number believed, and turned unto the Lord." This phrase, as in Ezekiel 3:14, "So the spirit lifted me up, and took me away, and I went in bitterness, in the heat of my spirit; but the hand of the LORD was strong upon me," and 2 Kings 3:15, "But now bring me a minstrel. And it came to pass, when the minstrel played, that the hand of the LORD came upon him," implies they were extraordinarily *called* and *enabled* to work miracles to *confirm* their ministry.

Objection IX. Apollos taught, knowing only the baptism of John, as stated in Acts 18:24–25, "And a certain Jew named Apollos, born at Alexandria, an eloquent man, and mighty in the scriptures, came to Ephesus. This man was instructed in the way of the Lord; and being fervent in the spirit, he spake and taught diligently the things of the Lord, knowing only the baptism of John."

Answer: Apollos was a *minister*, as affirmed in 1 Corinthians 3:5, "Who then is Paul, and who is Apollos, but *ministers* by whom ye believed, even as the Lord gave to every man?" He was an eloquent man, mighty in the Scriptures, and extraordinarily qualified by God for the work of the ministry.

Objection X. It is said in 1 Corinthians 14:31, "For ye may all prophesy one by one, that all may learn, and all may be comforted," (1 Corinthians 14:31). Therefore, we may preach.

Answer: The objectors are misled by the word "all" here. Who are the "all" referred to? Not all the saints, for women and children are saints, yet they may *not* prophesy. Rather, "all" refers to all the prophets in the church. In the renowned church of Corinth, there were many prophets, and some disorder arose in the exercise of their gifts. The apostle directs them to maintain order, prophesying one after another, not simultaneously, as stated in 1 Corinthians 14:29, "Let the prophets speak two or three, and let the other judge." What logic is it to argue that because ten, twenty, or more ordained ministers or prophets in a church may prophesy and preach one after another, laymen may also preach?

Objection XI. Hebrews 5:11 states, "Of whom we have many things to say, and hard to be uttered, seeing ye are dull of hearing," implying that for the time, they ought to teach others.

Answer: There is a kind of teaching that is the duty of every Christian, such as parents and masters instructing their households, or one Christian edifying another. This is the type of teaching, not *ministerial* teaching, that the apostle refers to in this passage.

Objection XII. Christians are a royal priesthood, kings and priests, and therefore they may preach.

Answer:

1. This description, found in 1 Peter 2:9, "But ye are a chosen generation, a royal priesthood, an holy nation, a peculiar people; that ye should shew forth the praises of him who hath called you out of darkness into his marvellous light," applies to all Christian saints—men, women, and children. Yet not all such may *preach*.
2. Every Christian is called a king in this sense, but does this mean they may invade the throne? The meaning is that every child of God is brought near to God to offer spiritual sacrifices of prayer, praise, and thanksgiving. This has no bearing on the question of lay preaching.

All the remaining objections are of similar force, proving nothing to the purpose. I grow weary of answering them.

Chapter 4: Ordination

Whether Ordination of Persons to the Ministry Is to Be Performed by Fasting, Prayer, and the Laying on of Hands?

Also Showing Where This Ordaining Power Is Lodged by Jesus Christ—Whether in a Diocesan Bishop, the People, or in the Hands of Presbyters?

Whether It Is Lawful to Hear Laymen Preach, and Related Matters.

Question IV. Is the ordination of people to the ministry to be performed by fasting, prayer, and the laying on of hands, or not?

Answer: In a *well-ordered* gospel church, it is necessary that all who are sent out to preach the gospel be *ordained* to that work by fasting, prayer, and the laying on of hands. I prove this with the following arguments:

Argument 1. Ordination by fasting, prayer, and the laying on of hands is necessary because all scriptural examples of ordination to divine offices in the church were performed in this manner, and none without it. As Mr. Clark observes, no example can be produced of ordination done otherwise; we have scriptural warrant for this practice, but none for neglecting it. In Numbers 8:10, it is written, "And thou shalt bring the Levites before the LORD: and the children of Israel shall put their hands upon the Levites." Likewise, in Acts 6:6, seven deacons appointed to serve tables—that is, to minister to the poor, an inferior office in the church—were ordained by fasting, prayer, and the laying on of hands, "Whom they set before the apostles: and when they had prayed, they laid their hands on them," (Acts 6:6). Similarly, in Acts 13:3, Paul and Barnabas, though extraordinarily gifted and called, were ordained by fasting, prayer, and the laying on of hands, "And when they had fasted and prayed, and laid their hands on them, they sent them away." This is also evident in Acts 14:23, "And when they had ordained them elders in every church, and had prayed with fasting, they commended them to the Lord, on whom they believed," and in numerous other passages.

Argument 2. We have an express command for this practice in 1 Timothy 5:22, "Lay hands suddenly on no man, neither be partaker of other men's sins: keep thyself pure." The negative command implies the affirmative: lay hands on suitable persons and no others. Just as the apostles ordained ministers, so must *all* ministers be ordained. Since the apostles ordained by fasting, prayer, and the laying on of hands, all who are ordained to preach the gospel must be ordained *in the same manner*.

Argument 3. If it has been the constant practice of the church, from the apostles' time to the present, to ordain ministers by prayer, fasting, and the laying on of hands, then this practice ought to be continued. This has indeed been the church's practice throughout history; therefore, it must continue. Mr. Calvin, in his *Institutes*, Book 4, Chapter 3, Section 1, after showing how the apostles ordained elders by fasting, prayer, and the laying on of hands, explains that the primitive churches, in their order and discipline, particularly in appointing ministers, *adhered strictly to the apostles' rules in their entire framework of church offices and governance*.

Question V. Where is this ordaining power lodged by Jesus Christ? Is it in a diocesan bishop, the body of the church, or the ministers of Christ?

1. It is certainly not lodged in a diocesan bishop, for, as previously proven, a diocesan bishop, as such, is not found in Scripture. Being merely a presbyter, a diocesan bishop can claim *no* superior power above other presbyters by God's Word, except what is granted by mutual consent.

2. This ordaining power cannot reside in the people. Although the people have the authority to elect and choose, as evident in Acts 6:3, "Wherefore, brethren, look ye out among you seven men of honest report, full of the Holy Ghost and wisdom, whom we may appoint over this business," they do not have the *ordaining* power. In Acts 6:5-6, "And the saying pleased the whole multitude: and they chose Stephen, a man full of faith and of the Holy Ghost, and Philip, and Prochorus, and Nicanor, and Timon, and Parmenas, and Nicolas a proselyte of Antioch: Whom they set before the apostles: and when they had prayed, they laid their hands on them," the people chose but the apostles ordained. Mere election to the ministry does not confer the office, for *nil dat quod non habet* (no one gives what they do not have). If there is neither precept, promise, nor example in all of God's Word of any people or church ordaining their pastors, *then the people have no such power*. Since no such precept, promise, or example exists, those ordained solely *by the people* are *not* ministers of Jesus Christ.
3. The ordaining power resides wholly in the presbyters and officers of the church. There is no

command, promise, or example in Scripture of anyone else ordaining. Church officers alone have authority from Christ to ordain others to the ministry, as Scripture abundantly demonstrates, such as in Acts 6:1–6, Acts 13:3, "And when they had fasted and prayed, and laid their hands on them, they sent them away," and Acts 14:23, "And when they had ordained them elders in every church, and had prayed with fasting, they commended them to the Lord, on whom they believed." This was the custom in every church and city, as confirmed in Titus 1:5, "For this cause left I thee in Crete, that thou shouldest set in order the things that are wanting, and ordain elders in every city, as I had appointed thee."

Question VI. Is it lawful to hear laymen preach? You have heard that they have no authority to preach; but may we hear them without sin?

How far it may be lawful to hear them when no ordained ministers can be heard is a doubtful matter, and I will not determine it here. However, to choose to hear laymen *when ordained ministers are available is a sin*, which I prove as follows:

Chapter 4: Ordination

1. It is the clear duty of every serious Christian to join as *a member of a particular church*, to *submit* to the pastor of that church, and to hear him *consistently*. This is evident from comparing several Scriptures, such as Matthew 18:17, "And if he shall neglect to hear them, tell it unto the church: but if he neglect to hear the church, let him be unto thee as an heathen man and a publican," Acts 20:28, "Take heed therefore unto yourselves, and to all the flock, over the which the Holy Ghost hath made you overseers, to feed the church of God, which he hath purchased with his own blood," Ephesians 4:11–12, "And he gave some, apostles; and some, prophets; and some, evangelists; and some, pastors and teachers; For the perfecting of the saints, for the work of the ministry, for the edifying of the body of Christ," and Hebrews 13:7, 17, "Remember them which have the rule over you, who have spoken unto you the word of God: whose faith follow, considering the end of their conversation... Obey them that have the rule over you, and submit yourselves: for they watch for your souls, as they that must give account, that they may do it with joy, and not with grief: for that is unprofitable for you." Christians must know to which flock or fold they

belong to receive the feeding and oversight of their pastor.

2. It is sinful to hear those for whose ministry we cannot pray for a blessing in faith, for we can *only pray for what God has promised*. Since *God has not promised to bless the preaching of those He has not sent*, we *cannot* pray for their ministry in faith.

3. We are expressly forbidden to hear such persons, as in Jeremiah 23:16, "Thus saith the LORD of hosts, Hearken not unto the words of the prophets that prophesy unto you: they make you vain: they speak a vision of their own heart, and not out of the mouth of the LORD."

Objection: Those were false prophets, but the laymen you speak against preach the truth.

Answer: Do they not claim that God sent them, when God never sent them nor gave them any commission? As it is written, "I have not sent these prophets, yet they ran: I have not spoken to them, yet they prophesied," (Jeremiah 23:21), and in Jeremiah 27:14–15, "Therefore hearken not unto the words of the prophets that speak unto you, saying, Ye shall not serve the king of Babylon: for they prophesy a lie unto you. For I have not sent them, saith the LORD, yet they prophesy a lie in my name; that I might drive you out, and that ye might perish, ye, and the prophets that prophesy unto you." The learned Chemnitius affirms that *none* are to be heard in the church *who are not sent by God*.

4. Furthermore, since laymen preaching is sinful, as has been proven, do you not, by hearing them, encourage them in their sin and thereby become partakers of it?

Would to God that weak, well-meaning Christians, who often have more zeal than sound judgment, would earnestly consider these matters.

Chapter 5: Member Duties

Showing the Duties of All the Members of the Church, Both Ministers and People, to God, to Their Pastors, and to One Another.

Having extensively discussed the nature of the ministry, let us now consider the duties of ministers, both toward God and toward the flock or church over which they are placed.

I. Ministers must be *skillful* and *well-instructed* in the mysteries of the gospel entrusted to them, as stated in 1 Corinthians 4:1, "Let a man so account of us, as of the ministers of Christ, and stewards of the mysteries of God." They must hold fast the faithful word, being able to exhort and convince those who oppose it with sound doctrine, as in Titus 1:9, "Holding fast the faithful word as he hath been taught, that he may be able by sound doctrine both to exhort and to convince the gainsayers." They must *rightly divide* the word, giving each their spiritual food in due season, as in 2 Timothy 2:15, "Study to shew thyself approved unto God, a workman that needeth not to be ashamed, rightly dividing the word of truth." Ministers must be *thoroughly* acquainted with the Scriptures and well-versed in the great doctrines of the gospel, as urged in 2 Timothy 1:13, "Hold fast the form of sound words, which thou hast heard of me, in faith and love which is in Christ Jesus," and 2 Timothy 2:2, "And the things that thou hast heard of me among many witnesses, the same commit thou to faithful men, who shall be able to teach others also."

II. Ministers are to preach the gospel, which is their great and primary work, as in 1 Corinthians 1:17, "For Christ sent me not to baptize, but to preach the gospel: not with wisdom of words, lest the cross of Christ should be made of none effect." This indicates that baptism, while important, was not Paul's principal task; *preaching* was his main *commission*, though he did baptize at times. Further, in 2 Timothy 4:1–2, "I charge thee therefore before God, and the Lord Jesus Christ, who shall judge the quick and the dead at his appearing and his kingdom; Preach the word; be instant in season, out of season; reprove, rebuke, exhort with all longsuffering and doctrine," ministers are solemnly charged to preach *diligently*.

III. Prayer is another essential part of a minister's work, as in Isaiah 62:6–7, "I have set watchmen upon thy walls, O Jerusalem, which shall never hold their peace day nor night: ye that make mention of the LORD, keep not silence, And give him no rest, till he establish, and till he make Jerusalem a praise in the earth." Likewise, Acts 6:4

states, "But we will give ourselves continually to prayer, and to the ministry of the word."

IV. Ministers are to catechize and instruct the ignorant in the doctrine of Christ, acquainting them with the form of sound words. Paul charges Timothy to hold fast to this form, as in 2 Timothy 1:13, "Hold fast the form of sound words, which thou hast heard of me, in faith and love which is in Christ Jesus." In ordaining others to the ministry, he instructs, "And the things that thou hast heard of me among many witnesses, the same commit thou to faithful men, who shall be able to teach others also," (2 Timothy 2:2). This is a *clear command* not only for parents but also for ministers to catechize children in the fundamentals of religion, as in Proverbs 22:6, "Train up a child in the way he should go: and when he is old, he will not depart from it," where the Hebrew *chanak* means to instruct or catechize.

V. Another part of a minister's work is to administer both sacraments of the New Testament—baptism and the Lord's Supper—as commanded in Matthew 28:19–20, "Go ye therefore, and teach all nations, baptizing them in the name of the Father, and of the Son, and of the Holy Ghost: Teaching them to observe all things whatsoever I have commanded you," and 1 Corinthians 11:23–25, "For I have received of the Lord that which also I delivered unto you,

That the Lord Jesus the same night in which he was betrayed took bread: And when he had given thanks, he brake it, and said, Take, eat: this is my body, which is broken for you: this do in remembrance of me. After the same manner also he took the cup, when he had supped, saying, This cup is the new testament in my blood: this do ye, as oft as ye drink it, in remembrance of me."

VI. Another part of a minister's work is to rule and discipline the church according to God's will. Ministers are *church rulers and governors,* and it is the duty of the church to honor and submit to them, as in Hebrews 13:7, "Remember them which have the rule over you, who have spoken unto you the word of God: whose faith follow, considering the end of their conversation," and Hebrews 13:17, "Obey them that have the rule over you, and submit yourselves: for they watch for your souls, as they that must give account, that they may do it with joy, and not with grief: for that is unprofitable for you." The key of doctrine and the key of discipline are committed to them, as in Matthew 16:19, "And I will give unto thee the keys of the kingdom of heaven: and whatsoever thou shalt bind on earth shall be bound in heaven: and whatsoever thou shalt loose on earth shall be loosed in heaven." The *papists* misuse this text to claim that Peter had authority over all apostles and that the pope, as his successor, derives the power to forgive sins from it. However, what is given to Peter here is given in the name of all the disciples, as seen in John 20:23, "Whose soever sins ye remit, they are remitted unto them; and whose soever sins ye retain, they are retained." Some interpret this binding and loosing power as the apostles' authority to establish binding ordinances for the church, while others see it as the power of church discipline granted to all pastors until the end of the world.

VII. Another part of a minister's work is to visit the sick, as in James 5:14, "Is any sick among you? let him call for the elders of the church; and let them pray over him, anointing him with oil in the name of the Lord."

VIII. Ministers are to comfort the feeble-minded, strengthen the weak and wavering, as in 1 Thessalonians 5:14, "Now we exhort you, brethren, warn them that are unruly, comfort the feebleminded, support the weak, be patient toward all men."

IX. Ministers are to teach not only publicly but also from house to house, as in Acts 20:20, "And how I kept back nothing that was profitable unto you, but have shewed you, and have taught you publicly, and from house to house."

X. Ministers are to be an example to the flock in pious affections and holy living, as in 1 Timothy 4:12, "Let no man despise thy youth; but be thou an example of the believers, in word, in conversation, in charity, in spirit, in faith, in purity."

II. Now let us consider the duties of Christians or church members:

1. Toward God.
2. Toward their pastors.
3. Toward one another.

We now turn to consider the members of a particular church, as distinct from their rulers and officers. These include all members of the church except the officers.

Now, I. Their duty toward God is expressed in the first table of the Law, which is to know God, fear Him, and hold fast to Him; to hear, receive, and obey His Word, to sanctify His name and His Sabbaths, to wait upon Him and worship Him in spirit and truth, as it is written, "God is a Spirit: and they that worship him must worship him in spirit and in truth," (John 4:24). To choose Him as our God, to follow Him earnestly, to delight in Him, and to love Him with all our soul, mind, and strength, and to place all our rest and happiness in Him, as it is written, "Thou shalt love the Lord thy God with all thy heart, and with all thy soul, and with all thy mind," (Matthew 22:37), and "Delight thyself also in the Lord: and he shall give thee the desires of thine heart. Commit thy way unto the Lord; trust also in him; and he shall bring it to pass," (Psalm 37:4–5).

II. The duty of church members toward their pastors and ministers; and these are:

1. To obey them in the Lord, as it is written, "Remember them which have the rule over you, who have spoken unto you the word of God," (Hebrews 13:7), and "Obey them that have the rule over you, and submit yourselves: for they watch for your souls, as they that must give account," (Hebrews 13:17).

2. To imitate their godly and holy examples, as it is written, "Remember them which have the rule over you, who have spoken unto you the word of God: whose faith follow, considering the end of their conversation," (Hebrews 13:7).

3. To pray for them, for their work is great, and their temptations and discouragements are many, as it is written, "Pray for us: for we trust we have a good conscience, in all things willing to live honestly," (Hebrews 13:18), and "Brethren, pray for us," (1 Thessalonians 5:25), and "Finally, brethren, pray for us, that the word of the Lord may have free course, and be glorified, even as it is with you," (2 Thessalonians 3:1).

4. To love, honor, and highly esteem them for their work's sake, as it is written, "And we beseech you, brethren, to know them which labour among you, and are over you in the Lord, and admonish you; And to esteem them very highly in love for their work's sake," (1 Thessalonians 5:12–13). The world hates, despises, and reproaches them; therefore you must love and esteem them.

5. To wait upon and *constantly* attend their ministry, for they watch for your souls, as it is written, "Obey them that have the rule over you, and submit yourselves: for they watch for your souls, as they that must give account," (Hebrews 13:17). If they are to be instant in season and out of season in preaching, you must be instant in season and out of season in hearing.

6. Not to hastily or rashly receive an accusation against them; the world is apt to cast dirt and reproach upon them, but you are not to hastily or groundlessly believe or receive what they say, as it is written, "Against an elder receive not an accusation, but before two or three witnesses," (1 Timothy 5:19).

7. You are to carefully examine and compare what they say and preach to you with the Holy Scriptures, rejecting what is contrary to them and retaining what

is agreeable, as it is written, "These were more noble than those in Thessalonica, in that they received the word with all readiness of mind, and searched the scriptures daily, whether those things were so," (Acts 17:11).

8. It is also their duty to flee false teachers who cause rifts and divisions in the church: all are to be regarded as false teachers who are not sent by God and commissioned according to the order Jesus Christ has fixed in His church, as it is written, "Now I beseech you, brethren, mark them which cause divisions and offences contrary to the doctrine which ye have learned; and avoid them," (Romans 16:17).

III. Let's now see the duty of church members one toward another.

Now the duties Christian church members owe to each other are:

1. To love one another and bear with one another's infirmities, as it is written, "This is my commandment, That ye love one another, as I have loved you," (John 15:12), and "We then that are strong ought to bear the infirmities of the weak, and not to please ourselves," (Romans 15:1).

Chapter 5: Member Duties

2. To endeavor to edify and build up one another in knowledge, graces, and holiness, and for that end to be often together in Christian communion, in prayer, repeating sermons, telling one another your experiences and what God has done for your souls, as it is written, "Then they that feared the Lord spake often one to another: and the Lord hearkened, and heard it, and a book of remembrance was written before him for them that feared the Lord, and that thought upon his name," (Malachi 3:16).

3. Another duty is brotherly admonition and reproof, which is to be done with much meekness, as it is written, "Thou shalt not hate thy brother in thine heart: thou shalt in any wise rebuke thy neighbour, and not suffer sin upon him," (Leviticus 19:17), and "Let the righteous smite me; it shall be a kindness: and let him reprove me; it shall be an excellent oil, which shall not break my head: for yet my prayer also shall be in their calamities," (Psalm 141:5).

4. Another duty is to be very tender of the church's peace, avoiding all causes of division and strife, as it is written, "Now I beseech you, brethren, mark them which cause divisions and offences contrary to the doctrine which ye have learned; and avoid them,"

(Romans 16:17). Maintain the unity of the Spirit in the bond of peace, not withdrawing or separating from the church in a light manner.

5. A tenderness and respect for the poor saints, the meanest Christian, as it is written, "There is neither Jew nor Greek, there is neither bond nor free, there is neither male nor female: for ye are all one in Christ Jesus," (Galatians 3:28). Yet this must not hinder our showing civil respect to men according to their age, office, or estate and degree in the world.

6. Another duty is charity to all in need, but especially to the poor saints, as it is written, "But to do good and to communicate forget not: for with such sacrifices God is well pleased," (Hebrews 13:16), and "Pure religion and undefiled before God and the Father is this, To visit the fatherless and widows in their affliction, and to keep himself unspotted from the world," (James 1:27).

7. To put the most charitable construction on the words and actions of others that they will bear, as it is written, "Charity suffereth long, and is kind; charity envieth not; charity vaunteth not itself, is not puffed up," (1 Corinthians 13:4), and "Charity

beareth all things, believeth all things, hopeth all things, endureth all things," (1 Corinthians 13:7).

8. Prayer for one another is another duty we owe, as it is written, "Confess your faults one to another, and pray one for another, that ye may be healed. The effectual fervent prayer of a righteous man availeth much," (James 5:16).

9. Another duty is to walk exemplarily so as not to give offense to the Jew, to the Gentile, or to the church of God, as it is written, "Give none offence, neither to the Jews, nor to the Gentiles, nor to the church of God," (1 Corinthians 10:32), so as not to open the mouths of open enemies nor grieve the spirits of those that fear God.

Chapter 6: Discipline

Of church discipline; lodged in the hands of the ministers of Christ. Who are to be owned and received as church members. What the power of the church is, in taking in, censuring and rebuking, and casting out such as do not repent.

The Lord Jesus Christ, who is the King and supreme ruler and governor of His church, has appointed a certain rule and order of church government to be owned, obeyed, and submitted to by all the members of the church; and those who oppose and resist that government Christ has appointed in His church, they oppose and resist Christ Himself.

Now, as the churches are *parts* and *members* of a nation or kingdom, so they are subject to the civil magistrate; and all the *members of the church*, whether ministers or private Christians, are, and ought to be, subject to the magistrates, for so has God commanded, as it is written, "Submit yourselves to every ordinance of man for the Lord's sake: whether it be to the king, as supreme; Or unto governors, as unto them that are sent by him for the punishment of evildoers, and for the praise of them that do well," (1 Peter 2:13–14).

But we are speaking of the church as called out of the world and separated from it, and incorporated together in a holy society to serve and worship God: and, in this respect, the church has peculiar laws and rules of government, distinct from the civil laws of princes.

The church is a spiritual society, governed by officers and laws of Christ's appointment.

I. In whose hands is the government of the church lodged?

Answer. 1. Not in the hands of all the people; that would be a strange confusion to have *all* rulers; Christ never gave the power of the keys to the whole church.

2. Not in the hands of a lay-chancellor, registers, surrogate, or apparitor; these are civil officers the Scripture knows not.

3. Not in mere *lay-ruling* elders; by careful inquiry into God's Word, there appears to me no such church officers who had a power to rule in the church *but not to preach* and *administer the sacraments*; the place so much pleaded for it, in 1 Timothy 5:17, "Let the elders that rule well be counted worthy of double honour, especially they who labour in the word and doctrine," seems to prove nothing to the purpose: for, as Mr. Fox notes upon the place, nothing can be thence concluded, but that as in the primitive times there were

many elders or ministers in one church, the work of preaching and ruling being distributed as they thought fit, but all having one and the same office.

4. But this power is lodged in the hands of the *presbyters and ministers* of the church; this is very plain from Scripture, they are called rulers, as it is written, "Remember them which have the rule over you, who have spoken unto you the word of God: whose faith follow, considering the end of their conversation," (Hebrews 13:7), and "Obey them that have the rule over you, and submit yourselves: for they watch for your souls, as they that must give account," (Hebrews 13:17). And to them the keys of church power and discipline are committed, as it is written, "And I will give unto thee the keys of the kingdom of heaven: and whatsoever thou shalt bind on earth shall be bound in heaven: and whatsoever thou shalt loose on earth shall be loosed in heaven," (Matthew 16:19). Neither is there any Scripture to show Christ committed this governing power to any other.

II. But what is the governing power given by Jesus to these church rulers?

Answer. It is a power given by Jesus Christ, and entrusted with the guides and officers of the church; to order, rule, and govern the church; and to administer all

Christ's ordinances according to the gospel. But here I only take notice of four things.

1. The power of admitting members into a particular church, and what manner of persons they are that are to be received and owned as church members: in this, as well as other cases, we must be guided by God's Word; I speak here only of members in full communion; and here let it be carefully observed, that such persons as were by the apostles and first planters of the gospel churches received, owned, and taken in for church members, are, by us, to be received and owned as such now, the rule to them and us being the same.

   Now the people that were the subject matter of the New Testament churches are called saints, as it is written, "To all that be in Rome, beloved of God, called to be saints: Grace to you and peace from God our Father, and the Lord Jesus Christ," (Romans 1:7). They were, many of them, so in truth, all of them so in profession; while persons make a tolerable profession of the Christian religion, not contradicting that profession by such allowed sin as will prove them no saints, we are bound, in the judgment of charity, to esteem them saints, though many of them may not be really so: so likewise the church of Corinth, as it is written, "Unto the church of God which is at Corinth, to them that are sanctified in Christ Jesus, called to be saints, with all that in every place call upon the name of Jesus Christ our Lord, both theirs and ours," (1 Corinthians 1:2), and "Paul, an apostle of Jesus Christ by the will of God, and Timothy our brother, unto the church of God which is at Corinth, with all the saints which are in all Achaia," (2 Corinthians 1:1), and "Unto the churches of Galatia," (Galatians 1:2), and "Paul, an apostle of Jesus Christ by the will of God, to the saints which are at Ephesus, and to the faithful in Christ Jesus," (Ephesians 1:1), and "Paul and Timotheus, the servants of Jesus Christ, to all the saints in Christ Jesus which are at Philippi, with the bishops and deacons," (Philippians 1:1), and "Paul, and Silvanus, and Timotheus, unto the church of the Thessalonians which is in God the Father and in the Lord Jesus Christ," (1 Thessalonians 1:1), and "Paul, and Silvanus, and Timotheus, unto the church of the Thessalonians in God our Father and the Lord Jesus Christ," (2 Thessalonians 1:1). In all which places you have either saints or church in such a place, which are synonymous phrases; the saints were the church, the church were all saints; that is, such who, having received the doctrine of the gospel and professed to own Christ as their Savior, were united in one ecclesiastical body for holy worship and Christian communion; though there were yet not only many imperfections in the best, but many who were scandalously guilty, as is very evident in the church of Corinth, in some errors in judgment, and their very undue approach to the Lord's table, as it is written, "For in eating every one taketh before other his own supper: and one is hungry, and another is drunken," (1 Corinthians 11:21). But we must not suppose these persons, known to be erroneous or scandalous, were so when first admitted, but afterwards appeared to be so.

Now, forasmuch as the Lord's Supper is an ordinance of full communion, only for such as are church members; therefore that person who has a right to sit down at the Lord's table has a right to church fellowship. Therefore let us inquire what is necessary to fit us for that ordinance, and the same will qualify us for full communion and church membership.

2. There must be a *competent* measure of knowledge in the doctrines and mysteries of the gospel; this knowledge must be especially in the fundamentals of the Christian religion, particularly in the person and offices of Christ, as it is written, "And this is life eternal, that they might know thee the only true God, and Jesus Christ, whom thou hast sent," (John 17:3).
3. The persons admitted must be such as are dedicated to Christ in the sacrament of baptism; such as have not received the first sacrament are not to come to the second.
4. Such as come to the Lord's Supper, or to full communion in the church, must solemnly renew and engage to *stand* to their baptismal covenant, that is, to repent of sin, to believe in Jesus Christ, to deny ungodliness and worldly lusts, and to live soberly and righteously in this present evil world, as it is written, "For the grace of God that bringeth salvation hath appeared to all men, Teaching us that, denying ungodliness and worldly lusts, we should live soberly, righteously, and godly, in this present world," (Titus 2:11–12). *A professed subjection* of soul to Jesus Christ, or of regeneration and holiness in

Christ's name, together *with a promise* of performing the duties of a church member to God, to our pastors, and fellow Christians (as before). I know no reason why such a person should be denied full communion, unless the person should be guilty of such known sin or disorderly walking as may evidence the profession he makes to be merely in hypocrisy: and, in this case, it is better to be too large in our charity than too censorious; for when we have done all, the heart is God's fort-royal, none but God can search it out: many that are unsound will yet have such a right to visible church membership, as that we shall not be able to keep them back. Now the whole church ought to be judge of the conversations of persons admitted; because they live among them and are able to judge.

But the officers of the church are the most meet and fit judges of their knowledge and qualifications for church communion, for they, by the ministry of the Word, gather and plant churches, as it is written, "Who then is Paul, and who is Apollos, but ministers by whom ye believed, even as the Lord gave to every man? I have planted, Apollos watered; but God gave the increase. So then neither is he that planteth any thing, neither he that watereth; but God that giveth the increase," (1 Corinthians 3:5–7).

II. Likewise the care of feeding, watching over, and rebuking, reproving, and admonishing belong to the pastors and officers of the church. Indeed the duty of rebuking and reproving belongs to all the members of the church, as is shown before; but especially to the officers of the church, as it is written, "And we beseech you, brethren, to know them which labour among you, and are over you in the Lord, and admonish you," (1 Thessalonians 5:12), and "Now we command you, brethren, in the name of our Lord Jesus Christ, that ye withdraw yourselves from every brother that walketh disorderly, and not after the tradition which he received of us," (2 Thessalonians 3:6).

III. To the officers of the church does it likewise belong to *debar* persons of church fellowship and full communion, that is, to suspend persons from the Lord's table, which is, by some called, the lesser excommunication; or, excommunicate and cast them out of the church, as it is written, "Them that sin rebuke before all, that others also may fear," (1 Timothy 5:20), and "Give not that which is holy unto the dogs, neither cast ye your pearls before swine, lest they trample them under their feet, and turn again and rend you," (Matthew 7:6), and "Of whom is Hymenaeus and Alexander; whom I have delivered unto Satan, that they may learn not to blaspheme," (1 Timothy 1:20), and "In the name of our Lord Jesus Christ, when ye are gathered together, and my spirit, with the power of our Lord Jesus Christ, To deliver such an one unto Satan for the destruction of the flesh, that the spirit may be saved in the day of the Lord Jesus," (1 Corinthians 5:4–5), and "But them that are without God judgeth. Therefore put away from among yourselves that wicked person," (1 Corinthians 5:13), and "And if he shall neglect to hear them, tell it unto the church: but if he neglect to hear the church, let him be unto thee as an heathen man and a publican," (Matthew 18:17).

IV. To the officers of the church likewise it belongs to revoke these censures, that when admonished, censured, or excommunicated persons humble themselves and repent, to admit them again to full communion, as it is written, "And I will give unto thee the keys of the kingdom of heaven: and whatsoever thou shalt bind on earth shall be bound in heaven: and whatsoever thou shalt loose on earth shall be loosed in heaven," (Matthew 16:19), compare with "Sufficient to such a man is this punishment, which was inflicted of many. So that contrariwise ye ought rather to forgive him, and comfort him, lest perhaps such a one should be swallowed up with overmuch sorrow. Wherefore I beseech you that ye would confirm your love toward him," (2 Corinthians 2:6–8).

Chapter 7: Schism

Showing what schism is, and when persons are guilty of it. And of consociation of churches and synods.

No religion can possibly more oblige those who profess it to unity than the Christian religion does. The Christian religion affords us very excellent helps, yet too many who profess the Christian name are sadly guilty of the breach of this unity, which is called *schism*. Schism is a causeless rupture or rending of churches or Christians in church communion, one from another. And this schism is either in the church or from it: a schism in the church consists in differences and dissensions between the members of a church; thus we find a schism in the church of Corinth, they differed concerning their ministers, crying up one above another, as weak or carnal professors use to do, as it is written, "Now this I say, that every one of you saith, I am of Paul; and I of Apollos; and I of Cephas; and I of Christ," (1 Corinthians 1:12). They looked more on the teacher than on the truth, and they had other differences about coming to the Lord's table, as it is written, "For in eating every one taketh before other his own supper: and one is hungry, and another is drunken. What? have ye not houses to eat and to drink in? or despise ye the church of God, and shame them that have not? What shall I say to you? shall I praise you in this? I praise you not," (1 Corinthians 11:21–22). As also concerning their several gifts, as it is written, "That there should be no schism in the body; but that the members should have the same care one for another. And whether one member suffer, all the members suffer with it; or one member be honoured, all the members rejoice with it," (1 Corinthians 12:25–26). This is a very great sin. Again, there is a schism from the church, and that is when an unwarrantable rent and separation is made from a church; when persons withdraw themselves from the church willingly, without any just cause, or for every light trifle. This is sinful schism when we leave a church where all the ordinances of Christ are purely administered, and nothing that is sinful imposed upon us; and so to leave or separate from a church out of giddiness or weariness is very sinful.

But, to depart from a church in which the great doctrines of the gospel are *overturned*, and *idolatrous* and *superstitious ceremonies are introduced*, and where we can have no tolerable comfort or edification, we may, nay, we must depart: separation in this case is no sinful schism; so that though the papists charge the Protestants with sinful schism for departing from the Romish church, yet the

Protestant churches have committed no crime in separating from Rome, but have done what was and is well-pleasing to Jesus Christ. For it is well proved, by many Protestant divines, that the church of Rome is mystical Babylon, a synagogue of Satan, and therefore it is the duty of all to separate from her, as it is written, "And I heard another voice from heaven, saying, Come out of her, my people, that ye be not partakers of her sins, and that ye receive not of her plagues," (Revelation 18:4).

But as to the separation among Protestants, not every separation is schism; we would not separate from the Church of England if we could avoid it, but there are terms of church unity imposed upon us, which we cannot comply with without violating our own consciences; we have studied, read, and prayed, and done all we can to satisfy ourselves, and the more we search the Scriptures and seek God's direction, the more we dislike the imposed ceremonies, and are brought to this inevitable strait, that we must conform against conscience, and so wound our peace, or be silenced, suspended, and thereby rendered incapable of public communion. We would gladly exercise our ministry in the public churches, were not the doors locked against us. So that we cannot, by any light we find in God's Word, look on ourselves to be guilty of schism; nor our people that willingly own and receive us as their pastors: and though we endeavor to have high thoughts of many that do conform, yet we look on those to be the schismatics who impose unscriptural terms of unity upon us, and thrust us out for not complying. There ought to be no more imposed on us than Christ and His apostles have made necessary to church unity, as it is written, "And they continued stedfastly in the apostles' doctrine and fellowship, and in breaking of bread, and in prayers," (Acts 2:42). We part with the church as a mariner parts with his ship in a storm. It is Bishop Bramhall's answer to the papists, says he, "If they did impose on us a necessity of doing sinful things, and offending God, and wounding our consciences, then we did not leave them, but they did drive us out from them." So we say we are not departed from the doctrine of Christ, nor any of His ordinances, and seeing they will not permit us to worship God with them without doing what we judge to be sinful, must we therefore forbear to worship at all?

Our assemblies are true particular churches, for where there are lawful pastors dispensing holy ordinances, and a people meeting and unanimously joining in the use of them, there is a true church. *Hic est fons veritatis, hoc est templum Dei, hoc domicilium Dei* (Here is the fountain of truth, this is the temple of God, this is the dwelling place of God), as

Lactantius speaks; what do our assemblies lack, except the controverted ceremonies? We read the same holy Scriptures, we preach the same holy doctrine, we have the same prayers in substance, though no liturgy, we have the same holy sacraments administered by ministers duly called and rightly ordained by Scripture-bishops: we have a great love and a very honorable esteem for churches and ministers that differ from us, if they yet hold the foundation: where, or what then is the schism we are guilty of?

II. Of the consociation of churches. The church of Christ, which is catholic (universal), being distinguished into lesser societies, that is, particular churches, and though these particular churches, being rightly constituted and organized, have the government within themselves, that is, every stated church has its own proper pastor or pastors, having full authority to teach and govern it in the name of Christ.

Yet there is a subordination of particular churches taken distributively, to an association or collective body of the same churches, whether there ought not to be a union or consociation of particular churches among themselves? Now it must be granted that particular churches are so many distinct members of one great body, that is, they are parts and members of the universal catholic church; and therefore being all united to one head, which is Christ, and all walking by one rule, the holy Word or gospel of Christ; they cannot but be interested in each other, and have a mutual concern in each other's well-being; as a particular single church for a provincial, and a provincial for a national church; and again, this national church for all other nations and churches abroad professing the same holy gospel of Christ.

And if the faithful pastor or one, two, or more pastors in a single church, by their holy diligence and wisdom, can advise what is most to the glory of God and edification of this single church; much more likely is it that an association of such faithful pastors, gathered together by consent from many churches, should be able to judge what is best for the whole.

III. Of a synod. And such an association of the pastors of several churches may be called a *synod*, when the pastors or deputies of several particular churches meet to advise and consult for the good of the whole: and that the unanimous agreement of the associated pastors is binding to all the churches whom they represent, provided their decrees are not contrary to Scripture, is evident, as it is written, "When therefore Paul and Barnabas had no small dissension and disputation with them, they determined that

Paul and Barnabas, and certain other of them, should go up to Jerusalem unto the apostles and elders about this question," (Acts 15:2), and "And when they were come to Jerusalem, they were received of the church, and of the apostles and elders," (Acts 15:4), and "And the apostles and elders came together for to consider of this matter," (Acts 15:6). But this question I leave to others who are better able to speak to it, as being beyond the design of this discourse. The conclusion: proving it to be the duty of every Christian to join in, and be a member of a well-ordered particular church.

    Now as a conclusion to the discourse concerning the church, let me exhort and persuade every one who loves their souls to give themselves to be a *member* of some particular well-ordered church. And I hope I have prevailed, when I have proved it your duty: now that every one ought to be *joined* as a standing church *member* to some particular church, I prove it,

1. Because those saints we read of in Scripture were *members* of some particular church, as it is written, "I commend unto you Phebe our sister, which is a servant of the church which is at Cenchrea: That ye receive her in the Lord, as becometh saints, and that ye assist her in whatsoever business she hath need of

you," (Romans 16:1–2). And "And if he shall neglect to hear them, tell it unto the church: but if he neglect to hear the church, let him be unto thee as an heathen man and a publican," (Matthew 18:17).

2. It was the manner of the apostles, that wherever God blessed their ministry to the conversion of souls, they still united them *into a particular church, ordaining* them elders to watch over them and feed them in the name of the Lord, as it is written, "And when they had ordained them elders in every church, and had prayed with fasting, they commended them to the Lord, on whom they believed," (Acts 14:23).

3. Christ commands us so to do, as it is written, "O thou fairest among women, go thy way forth by the footsteps of the flock, and feed thy kids beside the shepherds' tents," (Song of Solomon 1:8), in response to the church's plea, "Tell me, O thou whom my soul loveth, where thou feedest, where thou makest thy flock to rest at noon: for why should I be as one that turneth aside by the flocks of thy companions?" (Song of Solomon 1:7).

4. Because Christ is there graciously present, and where should we be, but where Christ is, as it is written, "And I turned to see the voice that spake

with me. And being turned, I saw seven golden candlesticks; And in the midst of the seven candlesticks one like unto the Son of man, clothed with a garment down to the foot, and girt about the paps with a golden girdle," (Revelation 1:12–13).

5. The titles and epithets given to the church in Scripture, it is called the house of God, as it is written, "For if a man know not how to rule his own house, how shall he take care of the church of God?" (1 Timothy 3:5). The flock of God, as it is written, "Take heed therefore unto yourselves, and to all the flock, over the which the Holy Ghost hath made you overseers, to feed the church of God, which he hath purchased with his own blood," (Acts 20:28). The terms plainly intimate that every believer must be an inhabitant in this house, a member of this flock.

6. The names given to ministers, they are called shepherds, overseers, as it is written, "Take heed therefore unto yourselves, and to all the flock, over the which the Holy Ghost hath made you overseers, to feed the church of God, which he hath purchased with his own blood," (Acts 20:28). Watchmen, rulers, as it is written, "Remember them which have the rule over you, who have spoken unto you the

word of God: whose faith follow, considering the end of their conversation," (Hebrews 13:7), and "Obey them that have the rule over you, and submit yourselves: for they watch for your souls, as they that must give account," (Hebrews 13:17). This proves they have a peculiar house, flock, to rule and govern.

7. The duty of ministers to their flock must suppose them to have some who are their peculiar charge, if we know not who are of our flock or house, how can we perform the duty of pastors to them, as it is written, "Take heed therefore unto yourselves, and to all the flock, over the which the Holy Ghost hath made you overseers, to feed the church of God, which he hath purchased with his own blood," (Acts 20:28).

8. The duties of people to their ministers, to submit to them, as it is written, "Obey them that have the rule over you, and submit yourselves: for they watch for your souls, as they that must give account," (Hebrews 13:17). And obey them, to love them, pray for them, afford them a comfortable maintenance, this they cannot do if they know not who are their own pastors.

9. From the end of the ministry; to instruct, edify, and build them up, as it is written, "For the perfecting of the saints, for the work of the ministry, for the edifying of the body of Christ," (Ephesians 4:12).
10. Every Christian is to partake of the ordinances, which he cannot do unless he be a *member* of some church, as it is written, "Thou hast commanded that thy precepts be diligently kept. O that my ways were directed to keep thy statutes!" (Psalm 119:4–5), and "There was in the days of Herod, the king of Judaea, a certain priest named Zacharias, of the course of Abia: and his wife was of the daughters of Aaron, and her name was Elisabeth. And they were both righteous before God, walking in all the commandments and ordinances of the Lord blameless," (Luke 1:5–6).

Appendix: The Supper

A Discourse Concerning the Lord's Supper

Appendix: A Discourse Concerning the Lord's Supper Wherein is shown, 1. The nature, end, and other aspects of the Lord's Supper. 2. That Christians now lie under greater obligations to attend frequently upon the Lord's table than the Jews did of old to attend on the Passover. 3. That a careless and causeless neglect of the Lord's Supper is a great sin, procuring great and sore judgments.

To the Christian and candid reader, especially my own flock.

The following discourse is the substance of several sermons preached upon this text, by way of preparation for the Lord's Supper. My aim, both in preaching and printing, is the same: to inform your judgments more clearly in the doctrine of the sacrament and to cure sinful extremes which many are guilty of. Some lay too much stress upon the sacrament, valuing too highly the outward work, as if merely receiving the sacramental elements has such a virtue in them as to sanctify the partaker and make him fitter for death and more acceptable to God than he was before. This is a great evil and borders too near the popish doctrine of *opus operatum*: this is to superstitiously abuse God's sacred institutions, to make those things appointed by God for our edification and salvation to be the means for our hardening and damnation; whereas the sovereign gospel ordinances, without such preparation for, and a spiritual frame and disposition of soul in their use, can do no good.

2. Another sinful extreme is that many well-meaning persons are, from time to time, kept off by a slavish fear of their own unworthiness; they stand trembling at a distance and dare not come: and yet, through grace, feel their spiritual sicknesses, their need of Christ to heal and bind up their wounds; they sincerely pant and hunger for Him, both to justify and to sanctify them, and yet cannot see that all the worthiness we bring to Christ is to see our unworthiness and be willing to be saved in a gospel way, as it is written, "Ho, every one that thirsteth, come ye to the waters, and he that hath no money; come ye, buy, and eat; yea, come, buy wine and milk without money and without price," (Isaiah 55:1), and "Come unto me, all ye that labour and are heavy laden, and I will give you rest," (Matthew 11:28), and "Blessed are they which do hunger and thirst after righteousness: for they shall be filled," (Matthew 5:6), and "And let him that is athirst come. And whosoever will, let him take the water of life freely," (Revelation 22:17). That

this may be a means of remedying these evils is the earnest prayer of your servant,
MICHAEL HARRISON

The Sermon

"But the man who is clean and is not absent on necessary business and forbears to keep the Passover, even the same soul shall be cut off from his people; because he brought not the offering of the Lord in its appointed season, that man shall bear his sin, as it is written, "But the man that is clean, and is not in a journey, and forbeareth to keep the passover, even the same soul shall be cut off from among his people: because he brought not the offering of the Lord in his appointed season, that man shall bear his sin," (Numbers 9:13).

God, having with a powerful arm brought up His people out of Egypt and led them as far as Sinai in the wilderness, now commands them to keep the Passover.

The Passover was first instituted in Egypt as a memorial of their present deliverance out of their Egyptian slavery; it was a sacrament of the covenant of grace, and it looked forward, pointing at salvation by the death of Christ.

Appendix: The Supper

Now the Passover, in its first institution, we have in Exodus 12. Wherein every family, or if the family was too small, two families might join together; they must take a lamb that had no blemish, upon the tenth day of the month Abib, which was the first month after the vernal equinox and answers to part of March and part of April; this lamb was to be kept till the fourteenth day, by way of preparation, and then to be killed, and with a bunch of hyssop to sprinkle the blood on the upper door-post and upon the two side-posts of the door; and to roast the whole lamb, and then to eat it in a traveling posture, that is, with their staves in their hands and their loins girded. They were to eat it in remembrance of their deliverance out of Egypt, and as a sign of the salvation by Jesus Christ, the Lamb of God, who was, in due time, to be offered up for them.

Now the Passover was a divine ordinance, and whoever did not make conscience to prepare themselves for and to worship God in it were to be cut off.

Now the case standing in this way with relation to the Passover, this occasions a case to be brought to Moses, in verses 6 and 7. Certain men who were defiled by the dead body of a man, so they could not keep the Passover on that day, came to Moses and said, *We are defiled; wherefore are we kept back that we may not offer?* That is, if we forbear, we are to be cut off; and if we come in this way defiled, we are to be cut off: *what shall we do?* Our text is part of Moses' answer, showing in what cases a man might be excused from coming to the Passover.

1. In case of legal uncleanness, which is by touching a dead body or any unclean thing. These must not come to the Passover until cleansed according to the law.

2. If any were absent upon needful business, forced abroad at the time when the Passover was celebrated, then he was excused; but otherwise, if not in this way hindered, it was a very dangerous thing to absent from the Passover; for,

3. He who omits or neglects the Passover, he shall bear his sin, as in the text, that is, the punishment of his sin, for so this phrase signifies, as it is written, "And Cain said unto the Lord, My punishment is greater than I can bear," (Genesis 4:13). So it is in the Hebrew: this neglect is a sin, and a sin that shall be rewarded back in the due punishment of it; and if the question is asked, What is the punishment of this sin? *It is answered,*

4. He who omits or neglects the Lord's Passover shall be cut off; now this phrase, to be cut off, imports either,
5. An exclusion from communion with the church by excommunication, which is a sore judgment.
6. Rather an untimely death to be inflicted by the hands of the magistrate, to whom God committed the execution of this, as well as of other laws. And lest any should complain of the severity of this law, a reason is given of it in the text, namely, because he brought not the offering of the Lord in his appointed season, that is, because they did not appear before the Lord and offer such sacrifices and perform such services to Him in that very season God commanded it.

Now the Passover being the second sacrament of the covenant of grace, and the great thing therein signified and represented being Jesus Christ and redemption by His death, I shall take occasion to speak of the second sacrament of the covenant, as it now stands, namely, the Lord's Supper; being, in substance, the *same* with the Passover; for the Passover lamb was Christ, as it is written, "The next day John seeth Jesus coming unto him, and saith, Behold the

Lamb of God, which taketh away the sin of the world," (John 1:29). As the paschal lamb was to be without blemish, in this it was a type of Christ, as it is written, "But with the precious blood of Christ, as of a lamb without blemish and without spot," (1 Peter 1:19). The apostle expressly calls Christ our Passover, as it is written, "Purge out therefore the old leaven, that ye may be a new lump, as ye are unleavened. For even Christ our passover is sacrificed for us," (1 Corinthians 5:7). Though the feast of the Jewish Passover has ceased, yet Christ, who was typified and signified by it, has come and has offered up Himself a sacrifice for us; and we are bound to commemorate His death in that way He has appointed: now, though circumcision and the Passover were taken down together with the Mosaic ceremonies, yet the covenant of grace, of which they were seals, is not taken down, but stands firm forever; therefore our Lord Jesus Christ, the head and King of His church, has instituted baptism and the Lord's Supper in their stead; baptism being the same to us which circumcision was to them, and the Lord's Supper being, in substance, the same with the Passover.

Now, as the gospel is more excellent than the law, so it does not loosen the reins and leave us at liberty to obey or not. But Christians lie under a higher obligation to submit to all gospel ordinances now than the Jews did to obey and submit to the ritual ordinances of that dispensation.

Doctrine: Such as causelessly forbear coming to the Lord's table do incur great guilt and provoke God to inflict upon them grievous punishments.

In speaking to this doctrine, I shall do these three things, I. Show you the nature and end of the Lord's Supper. II. That Christians have not only an equal, but a greater obligation to attend on and observe duly the ordinance of the Lord's Supper than the Jews had to observe the ordinance of the Passover. III. That a careless and causeless neglect of this blessed ordinance of the Lord's Supper is a great sin, producing sad effects.

I. Let us consider the nature and end of the Lord's Supper.

The Lord's Supper is the second sacrament of the New Testament, or covenant of grace, instituted by Jesus Christ in the place of the Passover, now taken down, in which by bread and wine set apart and received according to Christ's institution, His death and sufferings, together with all the benefits believers receive from Christ, are therein showed forth and sealed to such as in a right manner receive it; as also the worthy communicant does hereby solemnly renew his baptismal covenant and engage himself to Christ and His church forever. Here *observe*,

1. Jesus Christ is the author of this sacrament, as it is written, "And as they were eating, Jesus took bread, and blessed it, and brake it, and gave it to the disciples, and said, Take, eat; this is my body," (Matthew 26:26).

2. It is the second sacrament of the New Testament, or covenant of grace; baptism is the first and to be first administered: we are to receive the Lord's Supper, that are first baptized. And it is a sacrament of the New Testament, or covenant of grace, the tenure of which is, believe on the Lord Jesus Christ, and thou shalt be saved and thy house, as it is written, "And they said, Believe on the Lord Jesus Christ, and thou shalt be saved, and thy house," (Acts 16:31).

3. The Lord's Supper comes in the place of the Passover, as it is written, "Purge out therefore the old leaven, that ye may be a new lump, as ye are unleavened. For even Christ our passover is sacrificed for us," (1 Corinthians 5:7). Both of them directed *to Christ* for salvation, but with this difference: the Passover looked at Christ to come; the

Lord's Supper is a memorial of Christ already come and crucified.

4. The external and visible elements in the Lord's Supper are *bread and wine*, set apart by a *lawful minister* of the gospel, as it is written, "And as they were eating, Jesus took bread, and blessed it, and brake it, and gave it to the disciples, and said, Take, eat; this is my body. And he took the cup, and gave thanks, and gave it to them, saying, Drink ye all of it," (Matthew 26:26–27). Bread is the stay and staff of life; wine is one of the greatest cordials, and therefore the *best* to represent Christ and the benefits of His death.

5. The end of this sacrament is to show forth the death of Christ with the benefits of it to believers, as it is written, "And when he had given thanks, he brake it, and said, Take, eat: this is my body, which is broken for you: this do in remembrance of me," (1 Corinthians 11:24). That is, a sacramental sign of my crucified body, and "For as often as ye eat this bread, and drink this cup, ye do shew the Lord's death till he come," (1 Corinthians 11:26). And so likewise all the benefits of Christ's death, as pardon, peace, spiritual life, and increase of grace, as it is written,

"The cup of blessing which we bless, is it not the communion of the blood of Christ? The bread which we break, is it not the communion of the body of Christ?" (1 Corinthians 10:16).

6. Our engagement to be the Lord's; we in this solemnly renew our baptismal covenant and engage ourselves to Christ and His church forever, as it is written, "The cup of blessing which we bless, is it not the communion of the blood of Christ? The bread which we break, is it not the communion of the body of Christ? For we being many are one bread, and one body: for we are all partakers of that one bread," (1 Corinthians 10:16–17).

II. That Christians have not only an equal, but a greater obligation to attend and duly observe the ordinance of the Lord's Supper than the Jews had to observe the ordinance of the Passover. *The reasons are,*

1. The Passover was instituted by Moses, but the Lord's Supper by Jesus Christ; Moses was a servant in God's house, Christ was a Son; Moses was a faithful servant, so that there was a great deal of respect due to Moses, but much more to Jesus Christ, who was Lord and head of the house, as it is written, "For this man was counted worthy of more

glory than Moses, inasmuch as he who hath builded the house hath more honour than the house," (Hebrews 3:3). Moses was a servant, a steward in the house; Jesus Christ a Son, the head, Lord, and builder of the house, which is the church; so that there is a veneration, obedience, and respect due to Christ and to the institutions He gave His church above Moses; we are therefore exhorted to give the more earnest heed to gospel institutions, as it is written, "God, who at sundry times and in divers manners spake in time past unto the fathers by the prophets, Hath in these last days spoken unto us by his Son, whom he hath appointed heir of all things, by whom also he made the worlds; Who being the brightness of his glory, and the express image of his person, and upholding all things by the word of his power, when he had by himself purged our sins, sat down on the right hand of the Majesty on high," (Hebrews 1:1–3).

2. Because the Lord's Supper more clearly reveals Christ and salvation by Him than the Passover did. Polanus well observes that the sacraments of the New Testament do more clearly reveal Christ than those of the Old: it is true, the death of Christ and salvation thereby was the chief thing represented in

the Passover; yet the death of Christ and the benefits thereof are more clearly held out in the Lord's Supper. The bread very aptly sets forth Christ's body and His crucifixion in its breaking, and our eating it very aptly represents our union with Christ and spiritual participation of Him: so the wine very aptly represents the blood and death of Christ, and our being justified and redeemed thereby, as it is written, "And as they were eating, Jesus took bread, and blessed it, and brake it, and gave it to the disciples, and said, Take, eat; this is my body. And he took the cup, and gave thanks, and gave it to them, saying, Drink ye all of it," (Matthew 26:26–27).

3. The Lord's Supper is an ordinance under the gospel, the last and brightest dispensation, and therefore, as the gospel is more excellent than the law, so it calls for the more earnest regard, as it is written, "Therefore we ought to give the more earnest heed to the things which we have heard, lest at any time we should let them slip. For if the word spoken by angels was stedfast, and every transgression and disobedience received a just recompence of reward; How shall we escape, if we neglect so great salvation; which at the first began to be spoken by the Lord,

and was confirmed unto us by them that heard him," (Hebrews 2:1–3), and "He that despised Moses' law died without mercy under two or three witnesses," (Hebrews 10:28). As a New Testament ordinance is the highest and purest degree of gospel worship, so it is evident that the obligations of Christians are so much the *greater*, by how much more excellent the ordinances are, than they were under the law.

4. Because our preparations for the Lord's Supper are to be more solemn, and our attendance more frequent than theirs was at and for the Passover; *for*,

5. Our preparation for the Lord's Supper was to be more solemn than theirs was for the Passover. The preparation for the Passover consisted chiefly in certain external rites, as putting away leaven out of their houses, external purifications and cleansings according to the law of Moses. I do not deny but grant that all these legal ceremonial cleansings had a particular respect to the heart, and so the conscientious Israelites understood them, as is evident, as it is written, "Purge me with hyssop, and I shall be clean: wash me, and I shall be whiter than snow. Make me to hear joy and gladness; that the bones which thou hast broken may rejoice. Create in

me a clean heart, O God; and renew a right spirit within me," (Psalm 51:7–8, 10). But now under the gospel, these ceremonial washings and cleansings being laid aside, our preparation consists principally in preparing our hearts to offer up spiritual sacrifices to God, as it is written, "God is a Spirit: and they that worship him must worship him in spirit and in truth," (John 4:24). It is the spiritual uncleanness of our hearts, the leaven of hypocrisy, that we are to put away.

6. Our attendance on Christ in this ordinance must be more frequent; to the Passover they were required to come but once a year, but to the Lord's table we are to come often, as it is written, "For as often as ye eat this bread, and drink this cup, ye do shew the Lord's death till he come," (1 Corinthians 11:26). Intimating we should come *often* to the Lord's table.

7. The threatenings for the neglect of the Passover were temporal judgments; the soul that refused to come was to be cut off by the civil magistrate; but the judgments now threatened are more spiritual, a much sorer doom is pronounced against the abusers or slighters of gospel ordinances than those of the law, as it is written, "Of how much sorer

punishment, suppose ye, shall he be thought worthy, who hath trodden under foot the Son of God, and hath counted the blood of the covenant, wherewith he was sanctified, an unholy thing, and hath done despite unto the Spirit of grace?" (Hebrews 10:29). A punishment much more bitter than death, that has even hell and eternal damnation in it, as it is written, "For he that eateth and drinketh unworthily, eateth and drinketh damnation to himself, not discerning the Lord's body," (1 Corinthians 11:29). And an unworthy coming and careless neglect are alike heinous and displeasing to God; it is a despising of the gospel, a slighting of the last, best, and purest dispensation the church ever had.

III. That a careless and causeless neglect of the Lord's Supper is a great sin, producing sad effects. Now here I shall do these three things, I. Show what may be a just excuse to keep persons from the Lord's table. II. That a careless and causeless neglect is a great sin. III. What those sad effects are that a careless and causeless neglect is likely to produce.

What may be a sufficient excuse to keep persons from the Lord's table. When the providence of God has cast our lot in such a place where we cannot (though we desire) receive this ordinance, God does not require impossibilities at our hands. This was Joseph's case in Egypt, David's case among the Philistines, and is today the case of thousands in pagan countries.

When the state of the church where we live is so polluted, and this ordinance among others so defiled, that we cannot come to it without sin, nor have any tolerable hopes of getting any good by it, then we may be excused, as the church of Rome at this day. True, it is not every corruption in a church that will warrant our separation from this ordinance; but when the mixture of corruptions is so great that we cannot hope to get any good, God will make up the lack of it in another way.

When the Lord's hand is upon us in some bodily disease that renders us unable or incapable, either in body or mind, this will excuse us.

When works of charity or mercy require it. But now, setting these or what other things may amount to a just excuse aside, it is a very sinful and dangerous thing to keep away from the Lord's table.

None ought to stay away upon any pretext of worldly business, as it is written, "Then said he unto him, A certain man made a great supper, and bade many: And sent his servant at supper time to say to them that were bidden, Come; for all things are now ready. And they all with one consent began to make excuse. The first said unto him, I have bought a piece of ground, and I must needs go and see it: I pray thee have me excused. And another said, I have bought five yoke of oxen, and I go to prove them: I pray thee have me excused. And another said, I have married a wife, and therefore I cannot come," (Luke 14:16–20).

Nor do any ought to keep off from the Lord's table for any unworthiness in themselves; this is indeed what many plead, I dare not come, I am unworthy, but this is no just excuse. *For,*

Either you see your own unworthiness and are made sensible of the plague of your own hearts, and so are sick of sin, weary of it, your hearts being melted and broken for it; if so, this is your gospel worthiness, and you are the persons Christ invites, as it is written, "Come unto me, all ye that labour and are heavy laden, and I will give you rest," (Matthew 11:28). This is all the worthiness Christ requires of us, that we see our own unworthiness, that we are sick of sin, and willing to come to Christ as to our spiritual physician.

Or this is only a formal hypocritical plea, when you think rightly you have no right to this ordinance, but are in the gall of bitterness and bond of iniquity, under the power and dominion of your lusts, a stranger to any gracious renewing work upon your souls by the gospel; and not being willing to part with your sin, you only use this plea of unworthiness to prevent reformation, which you know must be in order to your being admitted to the Lord's table; you must not indeed come to the Lord's table in your sins, but you must reform, put away all sin, as it is written, "Let the wicked forsake his way, and the unrighteous man his thoughts: and let him return unto the Lord, and he will have mercy upon him; and to our God, for he will abundantly pardon," (Isaiah 55:7). So, "Wash you, make you clean; put away the evil of your doings from before mine eyes; cease to do evil; Learn to do well; seek judgment, relieve the oppressed, judge the fatherless, plead for the widow. Come now, and let us reason together, saith the Lord: though your sins be as scarlet, they shall be as white as snow; though they be red like crimson, they shall be as wool," (Isaiah 1:16–18).

Nor are we to keep away from the Lord's table under a pretense of the unworthiness of others; thus some will not come because they are afraid all that come have not grace. But,

Either these people you dislike are openly scandalous, they have the very marks of unregeneracy upon them, and if so, you are directed by Christ what to do in this case, as it is written, "Moreover if thy brother shall trespass against thee, go and tell him his fault between thee and him alone: if he shall hear thee, thou hast gained thy brother. But if he will not hear thee, then take with thee one or two more, that in the mouth of two or three witnesses every word may be established. And if he shall neglect to hear them, tell it unto the church: but if he neglect to hear the church, let him be unto thee as an heathen man and a publican," (Matthew 18:15–17). Go and tell him of it, lay his sin before him in the spirit of meekness; and if the first reproof gains him not, try it a second time, and if that succeeds not, tell it to the church, that is, the rulers and officers of the church, in whose hands the discipline is lodged, that they may deal with him. *Or,*

You only suspect them to be hypocrites, and yet can prove nothing against them; oh take heed of being too censorious of judging another's heart, when you find it so difficult to know your own; how much of this would be cured if we always put the best construction upon the words and actions of others, as it is written, "Judge not, that ye be not judged. For with what judgment ye judge, ye shall be judged: and with what measure ye mete, it shall be measured to you again. And why beholdest thou the mote that is in thy brother's eye, but considerest not the beam that is in thine own eye? Or how wilt thou say to thy brother, Let me pull out the mote out of thine eye; and, behold, a beam is in thine own eye? Thou hypocrite, first cast out the beam out of thine own eye; and then shalt thou see clearly to cast out the mote out of thy brother's eye," (Matthew 7:1–5).

Nor is it warrantable to keep away from the Lord's Supper; this is because we are *first* to give an account to the guides of the church concerning our knowledge and fitness for the sacrament in examination; this is what some pretend, they would come, might they come hand over head, and give no account of their fitness for this ordinance. *But let such consider,*

1. This is nothing but what you yourselves are willing to do in another case; are you not desirous, when you are sick, to let the physician know your case? You are then willing to answer such questions as he shall ask you relating to the state of your bodies; you do not think that one who does not know your case can administer what is fit and proper for you; and is it not most true and reasonable in the case of your souls? The ordinance of the Lord's Supper is not a converting ordinance, but only for converted believers, that is, such as in the judgment of charity we hope are so; and is it possible for us to judge

whether you have any title or fitness for it when you will not come to us?

2. What is it that we require of you but a credible profession of religion, a competent knowledge of the doctrines of the gospel, and a regular, well-ordered conversation?

3. Nor ought any to keep away because of the frequent return of the sacrament. It is an ill sign when persons begin to be sick of opportunities for their souls, to loathe this spiritual manna; we are to lay hold of opportunities, and when we grow slack or weary of them, it is a sad sign we got little or no good by them.

II. A careless and causeless neglect of this ordinance is a great sin. It is a slighting of an ordinance of God, and that is very dangerous. All God's ordinances are to be *owned* and *honored*; and this being a part of God's instituted worship, and God commands you to come often, if you never come or very seldom, this must necessarily be a great sin, as it is written, "And Jesus answered and spake unto them again by parables, and said, The kingdom of heaven is like unto a certain king, which made a marriage for his son, Then saith he to his servants, The wedding is ready, but they which were bidden were not worthy. Go ye therefore into the highways, and as many as ye shall find, bid to the marriage.

Then said he to his servants, But when the king came in to see the guests, he saw there a man which had not on a wedding garment: And he saith unto him, Friend, how camest thou in hither not having a wedding garment? And he was speechless. Then said the king to the servants, Bind him hand and foot, and take him away, and cast him into outer darkness; there shall be weeping and gnashing of teeth," (Matthew 22:1–2, 8–9, 11–13).

It is a sin not to come to the Lord's table because it is a *slighting of Jesus Christ Himself*: what a sin was it in the Jews to slight Canaan, that was a type of heaven? As it is written, "But they mocked the messengers of God, and despised his words, and misused his prophets, until the wrath of the Lord arose against his people, till there was no remedy," (Psalm 106:24–25). But much more to slight Christ, as it is written, "How shall we escape, if we neglect so great salvation; which at the first began to be spoken by the Lord, and was confirmed unto us by them that heard him," (Hebrews 2:3). In this ordinance, Jesus Christ, His death, and sufferings are represented to us; now, to neglect the death and trample under foot the blood of Christ must needs be a great sin.

Because the neglect of this ordinance shows great stupidity and unacquaintance with our own hearts.

But what are those sad effects produced by a careless and causeless neglect of the Lord's Supper?

Such a neglect *brings temporal judgments*; such as a blast upon our affairs, sickness, and death itself: and this not only the ungodly, but the saints themselves; God threatens, as it is written, "Then will I visit their transgression with the rod, and their iniquity with stripes," (Psalm 89:32). This was with the Corinthians, as it is written, "For he that eateth and drinketh unworthily, eateth and drinketh damnation to himself, not discerning the Lord's body. For this cause many are weak and sickly among you, and many sleep," (1 Corinthians 11:29–30). κρίμα (*judgment*, meaning any kind of punishment, either temporal, spiritual, or eternal, in this life or that to come); the Corinthians were sick, and many dead, and this was for contempt of the Lord's Supper; but these are too often overlooked; *but*,

2. Such a careless neglect of the Lord's Supper is often attended with spiritual judgments; as,

1. For such neglect, God often takes away the means of grace from them, as it is written, "Therefore, behold, I will utterly forget you, and I will forsake you, and the city that I gave you and your fathers, and cast you out of my presence: And I will bring an everlasting reproach upon you, and a perpetual shame, which

shall not be forgotten," (Hosea 10:11–12). It is a prophecy of the casting off of the ten tribes for their despising the ordinances of God; they slighted the prophets, and behold, they shall search the whole land for a prophet, but shall find none.

2. For such neglect, God leaves them to a spirit of unsteadiness, to be led away with the error of the wicked; or, they settle on their lees again, lose their first love, because lukewarm, lose their hearts in spiritual things, as it is written, "Nevertheless I have somewhat against thee, because thou hast left thy first love," (Revelation 2:4), and "I know thy works, that thou hast a name that thou livest, and art dead," (Revelation 3:1), and "So then because thou art lukewarm, and neither cold nor hot, I will spue thee out of my mouth. Because thou sayest, I am rich, and increased with goods, and have need of nothing; and knowest not that thou art wretched, and miserable, and poor, and blind, and naked: I counsel thee to buy of me gold tried in the fire, that thou mayest be rich; and white raiment, that thou mayest be clothed, and that the shame of thy nakedness do not appear; and anoint thine eyes with eyesalve, that thou mayest see," (Revelation 3:16–18).

3. Eternal judgments, as it is written, "For he that eateth and drinketh unworthily, eateth and drinketh damnation to himself, not discerning the Lord's body," (1 Corinthians 11:29). And may we not say, he that slights and neglects also incurs eternal damnation.

Application.

Is this so, that such as carelessly neglect coming to the Lord's table incur great guilt and provoke God to inflict upon them sore punishments?

I. Use. This shall be of reproof to four sorts of persons. First. This reproves those who look upon the sacraments of the New Testament as old, antiquated ordinances and of no use to Christians: are there not some who have thrown away both the New Testament sacraments under pretense of more spiritual attainments? Some will have no baptism but a spiritual baptism; nor no supper, but a feast within. It is indeed strange what such can say against plain gospel commands: Christ says, go, baptize, as it is written, "Teaching them to observe all things whatsoever I have commanded you: and, lo, I am with you alway, even unto the end of the world. Amen," (Matthew

28:20). These say, no baptism but that of the Spirit: and that holy apostle, Paul, must be brought in pleading for them, as it is written, "For Christ sent me not to baptize, but to preach the gospel: not with wisdom of words, lest the cross of Christ should be made of none effect," (1 Corinthians 1:17). So Paul did baptize; and, had it not been a divine ordinance, he would not have done it at all: but baptism was not his main or principal work, but to preach the gospel. And then, as to the Lord's Supper, the apostle tells us, as it is written, "For as often as ye eat this bread, and drink this cup, ye do shew the Lord's death till he come," (1 Corinthians 11:26). Not till He come in the Spirit, as the day of Pentecost, as some have weakly pretended; but, till He comes in the clouds of heaven to judge the quick and the dead at the last day.

Secondly. This reproves those who own and confess it to be an ordinance of Christ, yet seldom or never come to it, nor worship God in it: what have such to say for themselves? They will own that Christ instituted this ordinance, and that it is a duty to wait on Christ in it, and yet never come to it, nor ever take any care to prepare themselves for it: are not these persons very guilty, and even self-condemned? Read both our text and, as it is written, "How shall we escape, if we neglect so great salvation;

which at the first began to be spoken by the Lord, and was confirmed unto us by them that heard him," (Hebrews 2:3). Thirdly. This reproves those who, though they do come, do it seldom, rarely; once or twice a year serves their turn: the apostle says we must come often, as it is written, "For as often as ye eat this bread, and drink this cup, ye do shew the Lord's death till he come," (1 Corinthians 11:26). And they come seldom, very seldom; this neglect is a great sin. Fourthly. This reproves those who come, and come as often as the table is furnished, but come in a careless manner, without humble, pious, and solemn preparation: oh let such read and hear what the apostle says, as it is written, "For he that eateth and drinketh unworthily, eateth and drinketh damnation to himself, not discerning the Lord's body," (1 Corinthians 11:29).

II. Use of *exhortation*. Let me now speak, in the name of God, to every one of you; if you have any desire to partake of the blessings of the gospel or to avoid the judgments the contempt of God's ordinances will bring, then I beseech you to take this as a serious call from God to every one of you, to set about serious and solemn repentance and hearty reformation; and, as you love your souls, *consider*,

Without serious repentance and reformation, the sad effect produced by sin, and, in particular, this sin of carelessly neglecting the Lord's Supper, can *never* be removed, as it is written, "Let the wicked forsake his way, and the unrighteous man his thoughts: and let him return unto the Lord, and he will have mercy upon him; and to our God, for he will abundantly pardon," (Isaiah 55:7). Without this, there can be no hope of mercy: you must repent and be humbled for every sin; and, in particular, for this sin of slighting this blessed Supper, as it is written, "For if we would judge ourselves, we should not be judged," (1 Corinthians 11:31). That is, examine, accuse, condemn, find our sin, and condemn ourselves for it; and cast every small iniquity far from us, as it is written, "I hate vain thoughts: but thy law do I love," (Psalm 119:113), and "And I will pour upon the house of David, and upon the inhabitants of Jerusalem, the spirit of grace and of supplications: and they shall look upon me whom they have pierced, and they shall mourn for him, as one mourneth for his only son, and shall be in bitterness for him, as one that is in bitterness for his firstborn," (Zechariah 12:10).

You who carelessly neglect this ordinance of the Lord's Supper, you neglect others as well as this; this is not all you have to charge yourselves with; you dare not come to the Lord's table because you hear seldom, or pray seldom; or do what you do in religion *carelessly*; not hating sin, not examining your own souls.

Your neglect of this ordinance is a sad sign there are some sins you love and are not willing to part with; you have so much sense as to know, if you come to this ordinance, you must reform; therefore it is your darling lusts that keep you from the Lord's table.

A constant and careless neglect of the Lord's Supper proves you, in a great degree, strangers to the state of your souls. If you knew your sins and your needs, you would not dare, from time to time, to turn your backs on this ordinance.

This makes it too evident that you have no great love for religion, nor for Jesus Christ; if you had, you would not dare, from time to time, carelessly neglect that ordinance wherein the death and satisfaction of Christ, together with His great love in dying for sinners, is represented and held out to us.

Nor do you ever seal to your baptism, until you come to the Lord's table; in baptism, you enter into covenant, and at the Lord's table, we renew that covenant; now, to keep from the Lord's Supper from time to time is as if we did repent of our first entering into covenant and refuse to renew our covenant with God.

And therefore let me earnestly persuade you to prepare yourselves in an humble, pious manner for the Lord's table; do not mistake me, I am not persuading you to come hand over head, to come in your sins; but to prepare to come, to labor to fit yourselves for this ordinance; and that you may come to the Lord's table *comfortably*, Examine yourselves, as it is written, "But let a man examine himself, and so let him eat of that bread, and drink of that cup," (1 Corinthians 11:28). Now there are five things we must carefully examine ourselves about and labor to find in ourselves in order to our comfortable coming to the Lord's table.

1. We must have knowledge to discern the Lord's body, as it is written, "For he that eateth and drinketh unworthily, eateth and drinketh damnation to himself, not discerning the Lord's body," (1 Corinthians 11:29). We must know the *nature, end*, and *use* of the sacramental elements; and how Jesus Christ and the benefits of His death are here represented and sealed thereby.

2. We must examine our faith; whether we believe in Christ, and, by faith, feed on Him, as it is written, "Examine yourselves, whether ye be in the faith; prove your own selves. Know ye not your own selves,

how that Jesus Christ is in you, except ye be reprobates?" (2 Corinthians 13:5). And not a bare belief of the article of faith that Christ is the Son of God, the Savior of the world: devils and ungodly sinners believe that; but it must be such a faith as purifies the heart, as it is written, "And put no difference between us and them, purifying their hearts by faith," (Acts 15:9). And works by love.

3. We must examine ourselves concerning our repentance; a loathing of sin, hating ourselves for it, as it is written, "And they shall look upon me whom they have pierced, and they shall mourn for him, as one mourneth for his only son, and shall be in bitterness for him, as one that is in bitterness for his firstborn," (Zechariah 12:10). True repentance is a mourning for sin, a hating of sin, and a turning from all sin to God, as it is written, "Ho, every one that thirsteth, come ye to the waters, and he that hath no money; come ye, buy, and eat; yea, come, buy wine and milk without money and without price," (Isaiah 55:1).

4. Another thing to be inquired after in order to your coming to the Lord's table is whether you truly and sincerely love God, Jesus Christ, and God's people,

as it is written, "Tell me, O thou whom my soul loveth, where thou feedest, where thou makest thy flock to rest at noon: for why should I be as one that turneth aside by the flocks of thy companions?" (Song of Solomon 1:7), and "And they, continuing daily with one accord in the temple, and breaking bread from house to house, did eat their meat with gladness and singleness of heart, Praising God, and having favour with all the people. And the Lord added to the church daily such as should be saved," (Acts 2:46–47), and "The cup of blessing which we bless, is it not the communion of the blood of Christ? The bread which we break, is it not the communion of the body of Christ? For we being many are one bread, and one body: for we are all partakers of that one bread," (1 Corinthians 10:16–17).

5. New and sincere obedience to the gospel, as it is written, "Purge out therefore the old leaven, that ye may be a new lump, as ye are unleavened. For even Christ our passover is sacrificed for us: Therefore let us keep the feast, not with old leaven, neither with the leaven of malice and wickedness; but with the unleavened bread of sincerity and truth," (1 Corinthians 5:7–8).

Appendix: The Supper

This is what you are earnestly to beg of God to give, and when you find your hearts and lives in this way prepared, as that you can but say, in sincerity, that you hate all sin and are willing to leave it; and you do sincerely desire to believe in the Lord Jesus Christ, hungering and thirsting after union, communion, and likeness with Him and to Him, as it is written, "Ho, every one that thirsteth, come ye to the waters, and he that hath no money; come ye, buy, and eat; yea, come, buy wine and milk without money and without price," (Isaiah 55:1), and "Blessed are they which do hunger and thirst after righteousness: for they shall be filled," (Matthew 5:6). When you can love your enemies heartily, forgive, and patiently forbear injuries, as it is written, "Therefore if thou bring thy gift to the altar, and there rememberest that thy brother hath ought against thee; Leave there thy gift before the altar, and go thy way; first be reconciled to thy brother, and then come and offer thy gift," (Matthew 5:23–24). Mourning for secret sins, vain thoughts, deadness, lukewarmness, and indifference in religion; and resolving to live the rest of your days to the honor and glory of God, then may you come comfortably to the Lord's table.

This you are to do speedily, *delays* are dangerous; you are not to keep off from the Lord's table because you are sinners, but do as commanded, as it is written, "Ho, every one that thirsteth, come ye to the waters, and he that hath no money; come ye, buy, and eat; yea, come, buy wine and milk without money and without price," (Isaiah 55:1). Let the wicked forsake his way, and the unrighteous man his thoughts, and turn to the Lord.

Other Books by Michael Harrison at Puritan Publications

The Believer's Marriage with Christ

The parable of the Wedding Feast is explained in this excellent treatise by Harrison, demonstrating the Gospel offer of God to poor sinners, and providing assurance to those already converted.

Infant Baptism God's Ordinance

There is no better succinct, concise, precise and exegetically irrefutable work on infant baptism than Harrison's work. It is not just about baptism – it's about infant inclusion in the covenant of grace. It's about church membership.

Christ's Righteousness Imputed, the Saint's Surest Plea for Eternal Life

Christian believers have a hard time explaining their understanding of justification through the imputed righteousness of Jesus Christ. Harrison aids the reader to take a important doctrine, and make it simple to understand. It is one of his best works, and extremely valuable to the church today.

www.ingramcontent.com/pod-product-compliance
Lightning Source LLC
Chambersburg PA
CBHW032153160426
43197CB00008B/900